THINGS IN HEAVEN AND EARTH

AND EARTH

EXPLORING THE SUPERNATURAL

EDITED BY HAROLD FICKETT

PARACLETE PRESS
Brewster, Massachusetts

Library of Congress Cataloging-in-Publication Data

Things in heaven and earth : exploring the supernatural / edited by Harold
  Fickett.
        p.   cm.
    Includes bibliographical references.
    ISBN 1-55725-188-6 (hardcover : alk. paper)
    1. Supernatural (Theology)   I. Fickett, Harold.
BT745. T47   1998
230' .01—dc21

                                                    98-18983
                                                         CIP

Title page and part title illustrations
from paintings by Pat de Groot
"Provincetown Horizons 1998"
original size 10" x 10½"
oil on paper mounted on wood.

10 9 8 7 6 5 4 3 2 1

ISBN: 1-55725-188-6

Published by Paraclete Press
Brewster, Massachusetts
www.paraclete-press.com

Printed in the United States of America

CONTENTS

CONSIDERATIONS

REVELATIONS

CROSSINGS

INTRODUCTION

There are more things in heaven and earth, Horatio,
Than are dreamt of in your philosophy.
—Shakespeare, *Hamlet*

I LIVE WITH A DIVIDED MIND, poised between faith and doubt, longing for the heavenly and dismayed by its counterfeits. My condition is not far removed, I think, from that of most Westerners, whether we are skeptics or believers. At best, faith has always meant commitment on the basis of reasoned probabilities and experiences that are often difficult to communicate; but even these probabilities and experiences do not seem to count for much today. Living as we do in a global culture that takes its cues from materialism and regards God's role as unquantifiable and therefore irrelevant, if not unreal, we are prone to embarrassment when our thoughts lead to reverent and worshipful conclusions. It has always been hard to believe in a caring God. Today we almost feel ashamed to try. People who do not believe are the smart ones, we feel; people who remain believers must be stupidly obstinate. Almost every cultural image reinforces that assumption.

Some of the best writers of our time disbelieve, however, not in the divine but in our reigning skepticism. Their thinking can even credit the miraculous—the supernatural. Although embracing the supernatural is not an absolute corollary of religious faith, living in a world open to the possibility of God's intervention often accompanies such faith, particularly for Christians. From their writings I knew this to be true of the contributors to this volume, all of whom are Christians (although certainly the same subject might be addressed by writers of other traditions).

Readers will also know these writers to be thoroughly contemporary people, well aware of the doubting spirit of the age and its powerful arguments. The men and women collected here are hard thinkers and eloquent witnesses to their experience. They are not the kind of people who usually talk about such matters.

Why is that? This project began with the spiritual rumblings and discontents that led me to ask this question.

These days miracles often seem to belong to the worlds of tabloid journalism and religious hucksters, whether fundamentalist Christian or New Age. Televangelists dispense miracles via satellite hookup, and banks of psychics predict our futures over the phone. The angel fad has reached such dimensions we can now buy bath-oil beads that promise to confer the "scent of an angel."

No one wants to be classed as part of the lunatic fringe. A few of the authors I approached to write essays for this volume declined because they suspected I might be a clandestine member of a cult on a recruiting mission.

My sense of a need for this book came from the polite reticence that usually surrounds the topic. Two neighbors, one religious, one not, probably will not bring up the matter because they think they know where such a discussion leads. Even among theologians and clergy the supernatural acts as a dividing line that threatens to open up the ground beneath everyone's feet if not approached on tiptoe—or continuously straddled.

Yet if God did not visit the Jews on Sinai, if the Buddha's enlightenment came not from the numinous, if Christ could not possibly have been raised from the dead, then religion should probably fold its tents and tabernacles and leave the desert to irrigation projects.

Most people understand this yet do not want to imperil either their skepticism or belief through a close examination of the matter. But that is the purpose of written expression: to help us think through issues of human existence that are so powerful few among us can find the courage, will, and language with which to conduct an investigation.

An issue such as the supernatural cannot be left to charlatans and hucksters. Because it holds such importance for all of us, its investigation must be led by trustworthy guides—the best minds with the greatest linguistic gifts. The idea behind this collection was to ask such writers to articulate their own means of approaching the supernatural.

After I had invited writers to contribute, many found themselves having experiences that verified the topic's importance. An assignment the writer may have taken on as one among others began demanding a deeply personal response.

I received telephone calls asking me *exactly* what I wanted. "I want you to follow your own best thinking and instincts," I would say. My callers knew before I answered that is what they would have to do anyway; they always work in this way, which is why I approached them. They needed me to know, I suppose, that my own groanings of spirit had become theirs, and they wanted me to share their dark nights, at least for a moment.

Our writers eventually found their way out of their deprivations. They found themselves journeying through language to the supernatural's thresholds, to its boundaries and frontiers.

Quickly let me say this is not equally true of all the essays here. Some simply make splendid arguments for transcendent experience; see especially the pieces grouped in the "Considerations" section.

In most cases, though, our writers serve as guides to the places the natural and supernatural cross. They also comment on the forces that attract and repel these worlds, how they are glimpsed together or broken apart. Finally, our writers articulate why living in a supernatural world seems to be demanded of them; such callings are individual to each and all the more broadly appealing for their idiosyncrasy.

Within the human spirit lies a disturbing counter to cynicism—a strange and almost inextinguishable hope that God loves us, that God hears us, and that God acts as if he does both. At the very least these essays will mean something to those who have not stopped hoping. Perhaps this book will even have a role in making the supernatural a topic that can be examined without prejudice.

Harold Fickett
February 6, 1998

SIGNS AND WONDERS

MADELEINE L'ENGLE

KNOWING THINGS AHEAD OF TIME

IT WAS A HOT SUNDAY AFTERNOON, typical of North Florida in early September. We had spent most of it, my grandmother, my parents, and I, sitting on the porch which wrapped around the old beach house, slowly waving palm leaf fans, and listening to the waves slowly moving in and up the beach as the tide rose. Our palm leaf fans were real ones, made by my grandmother. In the church pews in the morning there were cardboard ones, with the name of an undertaker on the back. Good advertising. In those days before air conditioning the fans were essential, and for a long time the sound of church for me was the sound of the fans slowly swishing back and forth in the languid air.

I was twelve years old, a young twelve, a European twelve, still far more a child than an adolescent. We were just back from several years of living in France and Switzerland, and my father, though it was never said, had come home to die. His lungs, which had been gassed in the First World War, were slowly giving out. But the afternoon was quiet and peaceful despite the heat, which was strange to me after the coolness of the Alps. It must have been hard for my father, too, this humid heat. But this was my mother's country, and instead of wilting she bloomed.

During the afternoon friends dropped by, and this was part of the usual summer Sunday pattern: friends, mostly cousins, making the rounds of family after church, sitting on the verandah for a while, being offered palm leaf fans and iced tea. Toward evening a light breeze came up and eased the heat. I would have liked to go indoors and lie on my bed and read, but I was made to understand that this custom of Sunday visiting was a way to get reacquainted, or sometimes acquainted, with family.

We had a light supper of cold chicken and ham and salad, then resumed the Sunday visiting on the porch. The beauty of the ocean kept me from being bored.

Then we went into the house to go to bed. I said good night to my grandmother, to my parents, and went to my room. As I undressed and put on my light summer nightgown I was assailed by an intense feeling of oppression. Something heavy and ugly which had nothing to do with the weather wrapped around me. I did not know what it was. I knew only that something terrible was going to happen that night. At first I thought it might be fire, that the old beach house would burn down. But my subconscious mind shook a negative. I said my prayers, got into bed, and tried to read. I could not concentrate, and finally it came to me:

My grandmother was going to die that night.

There was no reason for this strange certainty to come of her death. I knew about death. Two school friends had died during vacations, and I shared the shock and lack of understanding of my classmates. But those deaths were distant. This one was next door, for my grandmother's room and mine were separated only by a bathroom.

My grandmother was well up in her eighties, and she had problems with her heart, but there was no reason to suspect that her death was imminent. She had seemed no more nor less herself that Sunday than any other Sunday afternoon. But I knew with a strange conviction that she was going to die. It never occurred to me to go in to her, though I could hear her getting into bed and turning out her light. My grandmother was a formal and private person.

I had said my regular nightly prayers, but I got out of bed and prayed. My name for my grandmother was Dearma, and I prayed, "Dear God, please don't let Dearma die. Please make her be all right. Please don't let anything bad happen. Please make everything be all right."

I prayed and prayed, got back into bed and read, turned off the light, got out of bed and knelt again, in the dark this time. Prayed. Please, God. Please. Please.

That was my pattern for hours. Into my bed. Onto my knees. Please, God, please. I knew that No is an answer, but I begged God to say Yes. And the strange oppression stayed wrapped around me like fog. I did not sleep, or even doze. I listened. Waited. Prayed. Listened. Waited. Listened.

Finally, about an hour before dawn, I heard a sound from Dearma's room. I got up, went around through the living room, and into my parents' room. Woke them. "Please go in to Dearma."

That was all I said. We went into my grandmother's room and she was breathing heavily and strangely. Stentorian. My father went to call the doctor. Came back into the room. The three of

5

us stood there and watched the laborious breathing slow down. Ease. Stop.

My memory stops there, too. I know that after the doctor had pronounced death my mother and I put on our bathing suits and walked down the ramp, across the beach, and into the ocean, into one of the most beautiful sunrises I have ever seen. I know this comforted my mother. We saw many ocean sunrises, but this was a spectacular one, in honor, she felt, of her mother's death.

And I said to God, "Don't do this to me. I don't want to know things ahead of time. Don't do this to me."

Mostly God has been kind. Prevision is not a gentle gift, and it can be abused when the person with the gift tries to foretell the future. When I knew that my grandmother was going to die I did not know anything that was not already happening. I simply was plugged into it a little early.

We drove into town that morning; I'm not sure why. Probably to arrange the funeral. But what struck me with amazement was that something extraordinary had occurred. Death had happened. And nobody on the streets knew. My grandmother is dead! I wanted to call out to them, and knew that it would mean nothing. How can anybody die and the earth not shake?

I like the old village custom of the church bell tolling for death as well as birth. Something important has happened. Notice it! Pay attention! You, too, were born; you, too, will die.

That night when I went to lie on the dunes I felt that the stars had more awareness than the strangers on the street. My grandmother was dead, and I did not know where she was. Somewhere, somewhere, she was alive in God's love.

This was not the first or only time God has revealed to me something I did not want to know.

When my husband and I were spending a month in China I was intensely worried about him, for no particular reason. I was deeply, darkly afraid that something was going to happen, that he was going to die while we were in China. When we got home I thought that I had been wrong, that this was a mistake on the part of my subconscious mind that sometimes knows things. But within two weeks he had been diagnosed with the cancer that was to kill him. Again, I did not know something that had not happened. When we were in China the cancer was already there, lurking in his body, ready to kill.

We all have many abilities that we have lost as we have settled for Western, pragmatic thinking. The first summer my husband, our baby, and I spent in Crosswicks, our old farmhouse in the Litchfield Hills, we felt totally welcomed. While we cleaned, painted, and wallpapered, it seemed that the house was breathing deeply, contentedly. At last, after a couple of decades of transient renters, real people who loved the house had come to take care of it. I was alone with our toddler a lot of the time, because my actor husband had to take jobs as they came up. I spent the baby's nap time writing what was to be my third book. I loved the house and felt loved by it.

But I also had an inordinate fear when I was in the car that I would hit a child. I am a careful driver. It did not make sense. But the fear was there. Then I heard that the husband in the family who had lived in the house the previous winter had hit and killed a child. My subconscious mind had been picking up on this fact.

To some extent we have to learn to shield ourselves. I find this to be particularly true in my apartment on the Upper West Side of New York where the night is punctuated by screams, sirens, gunshots.

But we are also missing a lot. Back when I was an adolescent at Dearma's house at the beach, I would go out in the evening and lie on the sand dunes and watch the stars and feel that they were shining down on me with an awareness of the love of the

Creator, and I would love them back with that same love. I still have that same wondrous feeling when I see the Milky Way streaming across the sky. Sometimes in church when I am at the altar and the host is put into my waiting hands I feel that I am taking the entire creation of the universe into myself, all the love of the Maker which is so great it is beyond my comprehension.

I was blessed with a mother I loved and who loved me and who lived to be ninety. After her ninetieth birthday she went downhill rapidly, mentally, her gentleness turning to anger, ordinariness into confusion. I had no prevision about her death, though I prayed for it. She was ready to go home, and keeping her here with her old brain destroying her was punishment, not life. For two weeks before she died the house was electric. One sunny day I went into my room, and across the room a light bulb burst into shards with no provocation. No one was near it. It was not turned on. The house was telling me more than I was able to realize in the business of trying to keep things going in a family of four generations.

When she died, it was immediate and painless. My teenaged son was carrying her into her room at the time, and he later said, "Grandmother was alive, and then she was dead. I don't know how I knew. But I knew."

And the house breathed a deep, long sigh of relief.

There are some people who are frightened by God's supernatural gifts, so frightened that they call them un-Christian or even Satanic. I have sometimes wondered if these people may not be among those who are deeply gifted, but in this world that demands proof, are unwilling or unable to accept these gifts. Afraid. The gifts are not unscriptural. To give only one example, Joseph was certainly gifted, and it got him into trouble before it gave him joy.

If we are willing, and if we accept the hard gifts with the gentler ones, we can regain some of what we have lost in what is sometimes called the supernatural world. Natural or supernatural, it is God's world, and in it we rejoice.

RON HANSEN

STIGMATA

AT SUNRISE ON THE FEAST OF THE HOLY CROSS IN 1224, a full month into a retreat of prayer and harsh fasting, the forty-two-year-old Saint Francis of Assisi knelt outside his hut on Monte La Verna and fervently contemplated Christ's crucifixion. We read in the *Fioretti*, which records his life and sayings, that Saint Francis became so inflamed with love that he felt wholly transformed into Jesus himself, when he saw a seraph with six fiery wings in front of him, bearing the form of man nailed to a cross. At first he felt fright, then joy at seeing the face of Christ, who seemed so familiar to him and kindly, but when he viewed the nails in his hands and feet, Saint Francis was filled with infinite sorrow and compassion. Christ talked to him for a good while, about what we are not told, after which this marvellous vision faded, leaving . . . in his body a wonderful image and imprint of the Passion of Christ. For in the hands and feet of Saint Francis forthwith began to appear the marks of the nails in the same manner as he had seen them in the body of Jesus crucified.

At first he tried to hide the five painful wounds—for his side, too, was pierced—but with his habit stained with blood and his feet so injured he could do no more than hobble, he was soon found out by the other friars with him. He finally allowed them to look with awe on the wounds in his hand. On the back the flesh was raised and blackened in the form of the head of an iron spike, and in the torn palm the flesh looked like the point of a spike hammered flat.

We do not know, of course, if Saint Francis of Assisi was the first person to receive the stigmata—the word is a Latin derivation of the Greek for tattoo, scar, or mark—but he is the first to have the gift of Christ's wounds inspected and chronicled. Hundreds would have a comparable experience through the next seven centuries, generally receiving the stigmata while in ecstasy, but in oddly differing ways.

Often, for example, their heads would bleed as from the Crown of Thorns, or mean welts would stripe their backs as if they had been lashed forty times as Jesus was. While in a trance, Elizabeth of Herkenrode, a Belgian Cistercian nun, would strike herself on the jaw and roughly yank at her habit as if she were being hauled like Jesus from the house of Annas to the house of Caiaphas, and on to the praetorium. A farm girl in Brittany displayed in the flesh of her breast the words "O crux ave," hail, O cross. Theresa Neumann of Bavaria bled frighteningly from the eyes. She and many other stigmatics seem to have had fairly healthy lives with no food but the Holy Eucharist. Wounds to the hands and feet have been formed like nailheads on occasion, but also have been holes big enough for an examiner to read the page of a book through them. In Louise Lateau of Belgium, Saint Gemma Galgani of Italy, and, in 1972, the eleven-year-old Cloretta Robinson, a Baptist, blood would ooze up in their palms while being observed by physicians, but when the blood was wiped away, no laceration would ever be found. A few have been bruised on their right or left shoulder as if from carrying a heavy cross. And Christ's wound from the centurion's lance journeys in size and shape, between different ribs, or from side to side.

Women are seven times more likely than men to get the stigmata, and those in religious orders far outnumber all others who have received it. Age seems not to matter: An eight-year-old French girl has been given the wounds, and so has a sixty-five-year-old Sicilian nun. Occurrences of it are far more prevalent in Europe, and in particular Italy, than in other countries, and Catholics so typically exhibit the phenomena that a stigmatic of another faith—there have been more than a few—is a genuine surprise.

Occasionally the stories of stigmata only fill one with pity. We read of a Mrs. H., a psychiatric patient in Australia, who claimed visions of Mary and wept tears of blood, but took her own life in 1963. Or Herr M., a businessman near Hamburg, a nominal Protestant who never went to church and whose stigmata were accompanied by intense headaches, confusion, and loss of weight, vision, and hearing. Saint Maria Maddalena de' Pazzi, a headstrong Carmelite nun in the sixteenth century, would tear off her habit and flamboyantly embrace a statue of Jesus while crying out in an orgasmic way, "O love, you are melting and dissolving my very being! You are consuming and killing me!" Aldous Huxley's history *The Devils of Loudun* relates the case

12

of Sœur Jeanne des Anges, the prioress of an Ursuline convent, who, frustrated in love, first exhibited a bloody cross on her forehead, was publicly exorcised, and then, obviously craving more fame, became a florid spectacle throughout France as she flaunted the names of Jesus and the saints written in blood on her hand. And the Inquisition declared that Sor María de la Visitación faked her hand wounds with paint, having been induced to do so by two Dominican friars who wanted the "holy nun of Lisbon" to augur hell for the King of Portugal unless he fulfilled their wishes.

If one reviews the Roman Catholic Church's hundreds of investigations of stigmata in our far more skeptical age, it is quite easy to find hoaxes, delusions, misinterpretations, and a host of theatrical, masochistic neurotics, or sincere people who have fallen prey to a forlorn and fraudulent piety. Only in a few instances has the Church ever ruled an occurrence of stigmata to be genuine, even then noting a variety of causes and extenuations, none of which have anything to do with the supernatural.

In Germany, in 1928, when the thirty-year-old Therese Neumann was attracting international attention with Christ's bloody wounds, with a lifelong fast that included no food beyond the communion host, and with visions in which she talked to Jesus in Aramaic, a language she could not have known, Doktor Alfred Lechler, a psychiatrist, took into his consultation a mentally ill twenty-six-year-old woman whom he called Elizabeth K. Working in his house as a maid, she was available for continual observation and hypnotic suggestion, and Lechler found it irresistible to try to have Elizabeth K. imitate Therese Neumann's feats. While she was in a trance, the psychiatrist told Elizabeth that nails were being hammered into her hands and feet, and the next day, he said, she manifested red and swollen abrasions. She was shown magazine photographs of blood welling from Therese's eyes, and within hours she was shedding blood-stained tears. Elizabeth K. even went without food for a week and, through Lechler's hypnosis, managed to gain weight.

Of course, the fact that functions and symptoms can be replicated does not mean they have fundamentally the same source. There is a world of difference between the fraught and uneasy lives of psychotics such as Mrs. H. and Elizabeth K. and the health and serenity of those stigmatics whose holiness was the conduit for wonders.

Look, for example, at the famous Italian mystic Francesco Forgione, who took the name Pio after entering the Capuchin order of the Franciscans at the age of fifteen. Ordained a priest in 1910, and forced to serve as a medical orderly during World War I, Padre Pio finally took up residence in the friary of Santa Maria delle Grazie in the village of San Giovanni Rotondo on the Adriatic Sea. There, on September 20, 1918, he was sitting in choir making his post-communion thanksgiving when he saw a heavenly light containing the form of Christ on the cross. Shafts of flame from the cross pierced his hands and feet. He wrote his father guardian, the Capuchin superior:

> I was suddenly filled with great peace and abandonment which effaced everything else and caused a lull in the turmoil. All this happened in a flash. Meanwhile I saw before me a mysterious person . . . his hands and feet and side were dripping blood. The sight frightened me, and what I felt at that moment cannot be described. I thought I should die, and indeed I should have died if the Lord had not intervened and strengthened my heart, which was about to burst out of my chest.

The vision disappeared and I became aware that my own hands and feet and side were dripping blood. Imagine the agony I experienced and continue to experience almost every day. The heart wound bleeds continually, especially from Thursday evening until Saturday. Dear Father, I am dying of pain because of the wound and the resulting embarrassment. I am afraid I shall bleed to death if the Lord does not hear my heartfelt supplication to relieve me of this condition.

The afflictions never healed, were never infected, and Padre Pio was soon famous. Hundreds of the faithful would line up to have him hear their confessions, or fill the pews for his Masses just to receive communion from his bleeding and half-mittened hands. Eminent physicians confirmed the authenticity of his wounds, but a wary Pope Pius XI—acting on misinformation, he later said—effectively imprisoned Padre Pio within the friary while the Church investigated the stigmata, a harassment that would continue off and on throughout his life. And his reputation only increased.

Whole books have been filled with tales of his holiness and miracles during the fifty years of his stigmata. Wild dogs were reported to visit the friary during his Mass, quietly listen to his voice, and at the *Ite, missa est* trot away. Mass with him would last three or four hours, so often did he fall into ecstasy during it, and he heard the thoughts of his congregation, offering their fears and prayers with his own. A hefty man, his only food was a few vegetables and a pittance of fish at midday, no more than three hundred calories. To a friend he confessed that the excruciating pain he constantly felt was only magnified if he slept, and so he did not sleep but prayed. Many claimed he was favored with the odor of sanctity, and wherever he went one could smell the exquisite perfume of a spice like cumin.

His was a gruff saintliness: He scowled at idiocies, chided whiners, hated television, brusquely answered most questions before they were asked, hotly refused to forgive sins that he knew were already confessed and forgiven, foresaw the future, fought with demons, healed people through touch, through ghostly visitations, through their dreams.

A teenaged girl with one leg in a thigh-high cast was horrified to find that her toes had turned black. Doctors feared she had contracted gangrene and would have to have the leg amputated. She appealed to Padre Pio for help and he touched the cast; when the hospital removed the hard plaster in preparation for surgery, the doctors were shocked to see that the formerly injured leg was fully healed and more beautiful than the other.

A baby girl was born who was such a grotesque and twisted mass of flesh that doctors did not know how to begin treating her. Signora Roversi, the mother, took the infant to church and dumped her in Padre Pio's lap, firmly insisting she would not leave until the child was cured. The girl grew up to be as supple and tall as an Amazon.

Humiliated on the field of battle, an Italian general was about to kill himself with his revolver when a friar suddenly appeared in his tent and shouted, "What on earth do you think you're doing?" The friar gently counseled him until the general agreed to live out his full life, but when the friar left, the general went out and upbraided his sentry for letting a priest get past him. He was flabbergasted to hear that no one had gone in or out of the tent. Much later, of course, he would find out that the friar was Padre Pio.

A farmer in Padova, three hundred miles north of the friary, was ailing with occlusions to the blood vessels in his lungs that no medical treatment could cure. Realizing he was dying, the farmer prayed for intercession and was surprised by a friendly apparition of a bearded friar who laid his hand on the farmer's chest, smiled, and disappeared. Completely healed, but so embarrassed by the weird circumstances that he told no one but his mother about them, the farmer went to a lunch months later and was amazed to find hanging on the wall of the house a photograph of a friar he had thought was imaginary. That night he journeyed south by train to San Giovanni Rotondo, to offer his gratitude to Padre Pio who, after hearing the farmer's sins in confession, asked quite naturally, "And tell me, what about the lungs now? How are they?"

In World War II an American Army Air Corps squadron leader disobeyed the order to bomb San Giovanni Rotondo because he saw the gigantic form of a friar in the sky, fiercely diverting the aircraft. He was chagrined to have to write about the incident in an official report. Worried that he had lost his faculties, the pilot found out about Padre Pio through offhand inquiries, and after the war visited Santa Maria delle Grazie, becoming one of Pio's "children."

One night the friars were awakened by hundreds of voices happily cheering Padre Pio, but when they looked in the hallways, no one was there. A friend asked Pio about it later and was told frankly that those were the souls in purgatory thanking him for his prayers.

Often he blessed holy gifts and, in a country with faulty mail service, packages. Once, however, shouting in wild anger, he forced a man to open a beautifully wrapped box. The friar then flung out its contents of books, holy pictures, and rosaries until he found hidden in the bottom a handful of lottery tickets. Tearing them into confetti, he thundered to his flock, "Get out! Get out! Devils, all of you!"

17

Karol Wojtyla, the bishop of Kraków, visited the friary in 1962 and in a letter written in Latin later requested healing for a mother of six who was dying of cancer. Padre Pio wrote back, saying the mother was free of illness, and as a postscript he noted that the Polish bishop would be the pontiff someday. Karol Wojtyla would be ordained Pope John Paul II in 1978, ten years after Padre Pio's death.

A friar companion said of him:

> He was living in another dimension, with one foot here and the other in the supernatural world. He maintained a perfect balance, and never let you know what was going on. One day, in this very hall, a woman whose son had recently died came up to him. She said, "Padre, please tell me if my son is in heaven." And he flashed back, as sharp as ever, "Why, yes, I've just come from there myself, this very moment."

A fool once told the friar that his wounds were caused by focusing too much on Christ's crucifixion. To which Padre Pio hotly suggested, "Go out in a field and stare at a bull and see if you grow horns."

Questions and requests of all kinds were brought to Padre Pio by the villagers of San Giovanni Rotondo: whether to buy a car, sell a home, change jobs, take as a husband this man, give away this favorite rosary. Will you heal my wife's tumor? Will you give my old mother just one more year? Won't you please make Papa quit the Communist Party? When will I fall in love?

Would he have become so famous, so necessary, were it not for his stigmata? Was it not a sign that attracted the faithful to him, who himself was a further sign of God's fatherly concern for the humblest things that trouble us?

In *Mariette in Ecstasy* I told the story of a passionate and attractive seventeen-year-old who in 1906 joins the religious order of the Sisters of the Crucifixion in upstate New York. At Christmas, the postulant's older sister, the convent's prioress, dies of cancer, and soon after the funeral Mariette Baptiste is favored with Christ's wounds. An investigation is begun within the Convent of Our Lady of Sorrows to find out whether Mariette is the real thing, or a schemer full of trickery, or a madwoman confusing sexual yearning with religious ecstasy.

Mother Saint-Raphaël, the new prioress, is troubled by the stigmata not only because Mariette's fame is hurting the tranquillity of the cloister, but also because she cannot understand why God would give Christ's wounds in such a way. Confronting the postulant in her infirmary bed, Mother Saint-Raphaël says, "I see no possible reasons for it."

"Is it so Mariette Baptiste will be praised and esteemed by the pious? Or is it so she shall be humiliated and jeered at by skeptics? Is it to honor religion or humble science? And what are these horrible wounds, really? A trick of anatomy, a bleeding challenge to medical diagnosis, a brief and baffling injury that hasn't yet, in six hundred years, changed our theology or our religious practices. Have you any idea how disruptive you've been? You are awakening hollow talk and half-formed opinions that have no place in our priory, and I have no idea why God would be doing this to us. To you. I do know that the things the villagers have been giving us have not helped us in our vow of poverty. And all the seeking people who have been showing up have not helped our rule of enclosure. And there are breaches to our vow of obedience whenever you become the topic."

She sees that the postulant is staring at her impassively, with a hint, even, of amusement. She says in a sterner way, "I flatter myself that I have been extremely tolerant and patient, thus far. I have done so out of respect for your late sister, and in sympathy for the torment you have in her loss. But I shall not suffer your confusions much longer. And so I pray, Mariette, that if it is in your power to stop this—as I presume it is—that you do indeed stop it." She pauses and then stands. "And if it is in your power to heal me of the hate and envy I have for you now, please do that as well."

If the fruits of stigmata are truly the esteem of the pious, hollow talk, confusion, hate, and envy, one may indeed wonder why God would grace the world with them. I do have some possible explanations. We are so far away from the Jesus of history that he can seem a fiction, a myth—the greatest story ever told, but no more. We have a hint of his reality, and the shame and agony of his Crucifixion, in those whom God has graced with stigmata. Conversions of life have come from them. We are taught the efficacy of prayer, the joy that can be found even in suffering, and the enormous, untapped powers of the human body and mind. That some who have been given stigmata are irreligious only confirms that they are favors freely given, not earned. That such a high proportion of stigmatics are women may be God's way of illustrating the importance of women in Christ's ministry and of correcting the imbalance in Holy Scripture, where a far higher proportion of men have their voices heard.

Cynics may find in stigmata only wish fulfillment, illness, or fakery, but the faithful ought to find in them vibrant and disturbing symbols of Christ's Incarnation and his painful, redemptive death on the cross.

I think of an English biochemist named Cecil who was in Italy when he fell asleep at the wheel of his car and woke up in a hospital, floating near death, his arms, legs, ribs, and skull fractured. A Franciscan friar walked into his room, forced him to confess his sins, gave him communion and last rites, and went away. Like others, Cecil would find out the friar was Padre Pio. Later, he visited Santa Maria delle Grazie and while the old friar celebrated Mass, Cecil felt transported to Calvary, as if he were really present at the Crucifixion. "I was utterly overcome," the Englishman said.

"Padre Pio made me visualize Christ's agony in the garden, with all its horror and revulsion.... He made me understand the extent of the pain and anguish, the price of sin and of saving souls. He showed me what the Crucifixion cost God—as far as any human being can grasp its magnitude."

We cannot grasp that magnitude, so it may be that God on occasion grants us witnesses.

PRINCIPAL SOURCES

Ian Wilson, *Stigmata* (San Francisco: Harper San Francisco, 1989).

Suzanne St. Albans, *Magic of a Mystic: Stories of Padre Pio* (New York: Crown, 1983).

A.G.
HARMON

AUTHENTICATING
A MIRACLE
THE CASE OF EDITH STEIN

Breslau, Germany. July 1893

AUGUSTE STEIN, MOTHER OF ELEVEN CHILDREN, stands in the doorway of her house. In her arms she holds her youngest child Edith, not yet two years old. Siegfried, her husband, is to set out on a trip, to inspect a stand of trees for his lumber business. He is in a hurry; the day is hot, and he is anxious to begin his hard walk into the woods, the only route to a destination miles from home. There is no time for long good-byes. But before Siegfried is more than a few steps away, the baby calls out to him. She raises her arms, her hands clasping, demanding that he come back. He laughs and embraces them both.

He is found later that day, sitting against a tree, deep in the woods, dead from a stroke. His wife Auguste will always remember their last embrace, and that it was Edith who brought it to pass—Edith, who was born on Yom Kippur, the Holy Day of Atonement.

Edith Stein would become a precocious child, one whose insights began to mature into an intense desire to know the truth, which she demanded of herself and others. Her mother, a devout Jewish woman who worked relentlessly to support the family, often remarked on this quality in the girl. Having lost her father, and essentially her mother as well to work, Edith grew demanding. At first, her family used her insistent nature as a game, a means to tease the child. Pretending to have said one thing, they delighted in watching her protest that they had said another. But when she grew older, and found that people were not always so strict in keeping their word, the game lost its flavor. Edith became confused and deeply sensitive. Tantrums were common; loneliness, a given. The way out of the dilemma, she decided for herself when barely more than a toddler, was the trustworthiness of the schoolhouse. She demanded to enter the first grade in mid-year, flatly refusing kindergarten. "In school," she later would say, "people took me seriously."

For the next seven years, Edith found the security for which she had been searching. She devoured her studies and was always at the head of her class. Her personality blossomed; she was mischievous, good-natured, and to her surprise, an excellent dancer—one who felt embarrassed whenever the mistress praised her grace. But at thirteen, she wanted to leave school; she was tired of her self-imposed severity, which kept her studying even while her mother brushed her long, black hair at night. Auguste, always indulgent of Edith, allowed the girl to take a trip to her married daughter's house in Hamburg. And over the next six months, while caring for three small children and doing housework, Edith developed another capacity, which grew alongside her quest for truth: a residing empathy, a need to serve others, which could pull her away from her studies. Even while writing her doctoral dissertation in philosophy, *On the Problem of Empathy*, she would take a leave of absence from the university to work at a Red Cross field hospital, nursing World War I soldiers at the front.

But if her search for reality was determined, it was painful as well. Though the family were devoted and observant Jews, Edith had lost her faith long before her superb intellect took her to the University of Breslau. Truth lay somewhere in reason, she felt, and reason was best understood in terms of the working mind. She studied psychology and history, but was disappointed at their inability to answer questions about human existence. Only after reading the philosopher Edmund Husserl's works on phenomenology, which focused on understanding reality through intuitive perceptions, did she find what she was looking for. Immediately, she took up graduate study under his guidance. Although fellow students included such renowned thinkers as Martin Heidegger and Dietrich von Hildebrand, Husserl considered Edith his best pupil; she won her degree with highest honors.

It was during graduate studies that she began to reconsider faith as a possibility, in part because of the influence of fellow students. Husserl's school of philosophy made inquiries into the "soul" and "being" respectable once more. "The barriers of rationalistic prejudice fell," she would later say, "and suddenly I was confronted with the world of faith. People I dealt with on a daily basis, people I looked up to in admiration, lived in that world." But in characteristic fashion, though truth and faith were no longer mutually exclusive, it was not until she had witnessed the two unified and integrated that her atheism "collapsed." Helping a colleague's widow put his papers in order, she watched intently as the woman drew strength from the hope of the cross. "It was my first encounter with the cross and the divine strength it gives those who bear it . . . Christ in the mystery of the cross." Truth revealed through suffering had drawn her, and she turned her careful, exacting gaze toward Christianity. In time she would say that her search for truth was a constant prayer, and that any who seek truth are in search of God, whether they know it or not.

One year later, her own search led to the defining moment in her life. At a friend's house on a weekend vacation, she discovered a copy of St. Teresa of Avila's autobiography. Intrigued, she took the Carmelite foundress's work to a chair and sat down. There, she read all day, all night. "That is truth," she pronounced the next morning. Her trials were just beginning, but the object of her search was now clear. And despite the understandable agony such a decision caused her and her family, she was baptized the following New Year's Day, 1922.

She also felt drawn to the convent, but for the time being remained in the academy, lecturing at universities throughout Europe. Studying Aquinas furthered her interest in science; it satisfied her to learn that the field could be approached from a standpoint of faith. She also wrote and spoke brilliantly on "The Ethos of Professions for Women," a work which would later influence Pope John Paul II's encyclical on the dignity of women.

Then in 1933 a Nazi decree required that Jews could not hold professorial positions, and she was dismissed from the University of Muenster. All obstacles to her religious vocation were gone, and she gladly entered the Carmelite convent at Cologne. There she took the name Sister Teresia Benedicta a Cruce—"Theresa, Beloved of the Cross."

For a time, she led a contemplative life. She wrote meditations on faith as a gift of nature, on its awakening a thirst for clarity, and on the mystery of its focus, the Christ Child. Her scholarly achievements flourished as well. Living what she understood to be a life devoted to the worship of truth, she completed her most famous philosophical works, *Finite and Infinite Being* and *The Science of the Cross*. At the urging of a Jesuit friend, Edith also began work on her autobiography.

With the rise of Nazi power in Europe, she was realistic about her chances of survival. Persecution of German Jews grew worse in 1938. After the horrors of Kristallnacht, she feared endangering the convent in Cologne. She transferred to the Carmelites in Echt, Holland; still, the persecution followed. Like other Jews, Edith and her sister Rosa, a fellow convert who accompanied her to Echt, were forced to wear the yellow star. Her privileges as a citizen, then as a human being, were increasingly denied. Edith always valued her Jewish heritage and proudly wrote and spoke of herself as a Jew. At the same time, she saw all unmerited suffering as united with Christ's. She wrote of sharing in Christ's suffering as a vocation that played an important role in God's redemption of the world. She sensed that she would be called upon to realize these ideas in her own life.

Though efforts were made to transfer Edith and Rosa once more, such measures became increasingly difficult. On August 2, 1942, in retaliation for the Dutch Catholic Bishops' public denunciation of Nazi treatment of the Jews—a denunciation wholeheartedly endorsed by Sister Teresia Benedicta—the soldiers arrived at the convent. They asked for Teresia Benedicta and her sister, Rosa Stein. For a moment, the other Carmelites were desperate, trying to negotiate the women's release. When the futility of these negotiations become obvious, Sister Teresia Benedicta turned and asked for her community's prayers.

"Come," she told Rosa, who was distraught and confused, "we will go for our people." She took her sister's hand, and they walked out of the convent.

"Being a child of God," she wrote, "means to be led by the hand of God, to do the will of God, not one's own, to lay all care and all hope in God's hands, to have no further care about oneself or one's future. Herein lies the freedom and happiness of the child of God. . . . But whoever has once taken this way, will never turn back on it again."

One week later, Edith Stein died in the concentration camp at Auschwitz. When last seen, she was washing the faces and combing the hair of her fellow prisoners, a group of Jewish children.

Brockton, Massachusetts. Saturday, March 21, 1987

Two-year-old Teresia Benedicta McCarthy is comatose. Her body has gone into multi-organ system failure: Her liver is dying, her kidneys are failing, and her brain stem is swelling, all due to the accidental ingestion of a pain reliever in a dosage at least sixteen times the toxicity level for a child her age. She has not responded to any treatment administered by the staff of Massachusetts General Hospital, one of America's finest medical institutions. Her urgent status has doctors discussing an immediate liver transplant. Without such measures, her death is probable; even with them, her chances of survival do not exceed fifty percent.

Five days later, Thursday, March 26, 1987

Benedicta McCarthy's kidneys are functioning normally. Although she has not received a transplant, her liver has regenerated, reducing from five times the size of that of an average two year-old to normal. She is alert and active. By the end of the week, her health's reversal is complete. She walks out of the hospital with a balloon and pushes the elevator button herself. Dr.

Ronald Kleinman, attending physician, pediatric gastroenterologist at Mass General, professor at Harvard Medical School, states that he has never seen a child so sick and unresponsive recover so quickly and completely.

Between these two dates, at five o'clock in the afternoon on Sunday, March 22, the child's mother, Mary McCarthy, entered the hospital room, placed her hands on Benedicta's abdomen, and asked God to heal her child. She asked that he do so through the intercession of the child's patron and namesake, Sister Teresia Benedicta of the Cross—Edith Stein. Little Benedicta McCarthy had been born on the eve of the forty-third anniversary of her patron's death at Auschwitz.

Of all that modern religion finds difficult, miracles certainly must be the most trying. Miracles, after all, are embarrassing. They are disconcerting and frightening, even for the believer. People often cry out for concrete evidence of God's care, some assurance that our prayers do not stop at the roof; but how many of us would be profoundly disturbed upon receiving such answers? We might have to tell somebody, and then what?

Nevertheless, many people do tell about such experiences, and it seems a great many contemporary people want them to. Perhaps we harbor a small diffident desire to see whether there really is something inexplicable to experts: something, somewhere, that someone has not already figured out. And it is with that interest that we can examine the events in Brockton, Massachusetts. They already have been examined, in fact—scientifically, and with a healthy dose of skepticism—through an elaborate, bureaucratic process of the Roman Catholic Church. Little Benedicta's healing came under review in determining

whether Edith Stein—Teresia Benedicta of the Cross—should
be venerated as a saint.

In the Catholic tradition, the saint is a member of the communion of saints, which connects all believers in this world and
the world to come. Saints are believed to pray for those still on
earth: They *intercede* with God on our behalf. Throughout the
history of the Church, people have honored some particular
deceased individual who has acquired a reputation for exceptional holiness and virtue. Though at first such recognition was
at the grass-roots level, by as early as the twelfth century the
Catholic Church had instituted a formal process for the examination of potential saints. The process has grown increasingly
strict over the centuries, with additions and changes, but in its
present state involves the following procedure.

Groups who seek the Church's public recognition of an individual must solicit the bishop of their diocese to open a formal
effort, known as a *cause*, on the individual's behalf. If the bishop
agrees, he must then commission a tribunal to investigate the
individual's life, gathering all information, testimony, writings,
and other such documentation, regarding the person's reputation for holiness. The effort often takes years, but when all is
accomplished, the information is sent to Rome. There it is
examined by a branch of the Vatican known as the Congregation
for the Causes of Saints. If the Congregation finds nothing
objectionable in the information, the cause continues under an
appointed Postulator General, who acts as a coordinator of the
process. After years of examining the person's life and works, the
individual—known throughout as "the Servant of God"—may
be proclaimed to have lived a heroically virtuous life, and honored with the title "Venerable."

But the cause is not done yet. Sainthood is the Church's official recognition that an individual is in the presence of God, and

for such a proclamation to be made, divine signs are required in the form of miracles. The potential saint must, in effect, send back news from heaven, interceding for the faithful who ask for prayers. In most cases, two authenticated miracles must be attributed to the intercession of the person in question: one for the cause to proceed to the stage of beatification, after which the title "Blessed" precedes the Servant's name (a beatified individual is honored only in a limited area, such as his home diocese or country), and one more before canonization, which means that the Servant is known as "Saint" and is honored by the universal church. In the case of martyrs, however, no miracle is necessary for beatification. An authenticated miracle is still required for the martyr's canonization.

Of course, throughout history there have been countless stories of miracles, in which the faithful on earth are said to have asked and received assistance from the faithful in God's presence. These claims include, among other things, cures, rescues, and the realization of goals. Certainly, many ancient stories are more legend than truth, and it is important to say that the authentication of a medical miracle today, because of the advances of modern science, is much more difficult to establish than in times past. The Church has nothing to gain, and everything to lose, by attributing the miraculous to the suspect. All documents and testimony from any cause are kept in the Vatican archives; as they are subject to public perusal, they are consequently subject to history's judgment. For this reason, the examination process is rigorous. The burden of proof rests squarely on the shoulders of the cause. According to Fr. Kieran Kavanaugh, a Discalced Carmelite friar closely involved in the McCarthy case, it takes a miracle to get a miracle approved in the Catholic Church today.

Fr. Kieran, a quiet, sixty-nine-year-old scholar, has devoted much of his life to the great spiritual works of his order, including translating *The Collected Works of St. John of the Cross*, and *The Collected Works of St. Teresa of Avila*. He became involved with the events in Brockton in 1991, while on a trip to Rome for a meeting. Fr. Kieran received a call from Father Simeone of the Holy Family, a fellow Carmelite who lives in Rome and functions as the Postulator General for many cases. Fr. Simeone contacted Fr. Kieran about the events in Brockton. They had been suggested for review in the *cause* of Sister Teresia Benedicta, which had been instituted in 1962.

Of course, Fr. Kieran was familiar with the nun, both as a philosopher and a member of his own order, long before Fr. Simeone contacted him. But he had no idea in 1991 how intimately involved he was to become in the cause for sainthood. Four years before, in the spring of 1987, Sister Teresia Benedicta had been beatified. The beatification followed the events of the McCarthy case by only two months. The healing had received some media coverage and had come to Fr. Simeone's attention through a magazine story. Any cause receives many reports of miracles, but the Postulator's experience in such matters tells him which events bear a preliminary investigation; the Brockton event was promising. Fr. Simeone wanted Fr. Kieran to be Vice Postulator for the cause, entrusted with the duties of gathering all pertinent information. The Congregation of Saints requires that the tribunal, as the inquiring body is known, be seated in the diocese where the supposed miracle occurred. Since Fr. Kieran lived in Boston at the time, he was the natural choice for the job.

Before any witnesses could be called, testimony gathered, medical records collected, or slides, X-rays, and lab reports assembled, Fr. Kieran had to make sure the tribunal followed prescribed procedure to the letter. Protocol is exact and strictly enforced, says Fr. Kieran, as he can illustrate by the notebook full of procedures necessary for opening and operating the inquiry. The first thing that the Congregation of Saints pores over is whether a tribunal followed proper procedure; if it did not, the entire body of work—which can take months or years to amass—is sent back and the tribunal must start over. Understandably, there is great incentive to do it right.

First, the bishop of the diocese must conduct an opening session, in which members of the tribunal are appointed. Cardinal Bernard Law, the Archbishop of the Diocese of Boston, conducted the opening session in 1992, designating the following tribunal members for the McCarthy case: a judge, in the person of the Cardinal's Vicar General, Monsignor Robert Deeley, who presided over each meeting; a promoter of justice, Father Michael Foster, who with the judge asked questions of witnesses; a notary, who transcribed all oral testimony and officially notarized each of the eight hundred pages of documents; the Vice Postulator, Fr. Kieran, who prepared questions for witnesses; and a physician, who helped Fr. Kieran prepare appropriate medical questions for the doctors, nurses, and other medical personnel. Dr. James F. McDonough, former editor of *The New England Journal of Medicine*, served in this capacity.

Fr. Kieran and the other tribunal members had to solicit answers relevant to three lines of inquiry: (1) the seriousness of the illness, (2) the specific invocation of the Servant of God, and (3) the inexplicability of the cure. It is never the tribunal's job to pass judgment on any of the information gathered; that decision is left to the Congregation of Saints. Rather, the tribunal must accumulate all the facts and data, both positive and negative, so that an informed decision can be made once the case gets to Rome.

For purposes of establishing both the seriousness of the illness as well as the invocation of the Servant of God, key witnesses included Benedicta's parents and several members of her family. Each witness testified alone, under oath, while the notary transcribed the statement for inclusion in the *positio*, the accumulated data concerning the case. The tribunal solicited answers as to the family's familiarity with Blessed Teresia Benedicta and their memory of the events that transpired during the end of March 1987.

Little Benedicta's father, Charles McCarthy, is a Catholic priest of the Melkite rite, an Eastern tradition that permits its priests to marry. A lawyer, philosopher, and peace activist, he testified that he had grown devoted to Edith Stein through her writings. In his studies, he happened to learn that the nun had died at Auschwitz on the same day that he was ordained a priest: August 9. When his twelfth child was born at 7:45 PM, August 8, 1984 (1:45 AM, August 9, Auschwitz time), he and his wife named her for the philosopher-nun. Two days after Benedicta's birth, as it happened, the Edith Stein Guild was belatedly observing an anniversary mass at St. Patrick's Cathedral in New York, at which Fr. McCarthy was a concelebrant. When the Guild heard of Fr. McCarthy's new child, they made Benedicta a lifetime member and awarded her with their honorary medal, a cross superimposed on the Star of David.

Concerning the events themselves Fr. McCarthy recalled that during the week of March 15, he and his wife were on a retreat, leaving their older, college-age children in charge. It was the parents' first time away from home alone in all their years as parents. Checking in every night, Mrs. McCarthy learned early in the week that some of the younger children—but not Benedicta— had come down with the flu. When asked by one of her daughters, she explained where they could find packets of Extra-Strength Tylenol.

On Friday, March 20, when the McCarthys returned home, they were met outside by their oldest daughters, who frantically told them that Benedicta was at Cardinal Cushing Hospital. Thinking that the increasingly sluggish, unfocused child had caught the flu, the girls had taken her to the emergency room. Once there, however, they learned that Benedicta had ingested sixteen times the toxic level of acetaminophen, the active agent in Tylenol. Without anyone's knowledge, the child had apparently found the packets and had been taking the drug over several days as though it were candy. Fr. McCarthy testified that at 7:30 PM that night, his daughter was unresponsive and catatonic. Benedicta was transferred that night to Massachusetts General Hospital, which had a greater capacity to deal with such poisonings.

As Mass General's staff prepared his child to undergo treatment, Fr. McCarthy pinned Benedicta's Edith Stein medal to her pillow.

The girl's condition grew worse the next day, Saturday, March 21. The tribunal solicited the testimony of Dr. Ronald Kleinman, pediatric gastroenterologist at Mass General, to explain the gravity of her condition at this time. Dr. Kleinman, himself Jewish, was not familiar with Edith Stein before the tribunal called him to testify. His testimony was limited to medical events.

When taken in large doses, acetaminophen has a destructive effect on the liver, the organ that filters blood of impurities. As the body metabolizes toxic doses of the drug, the liver's functioning becomes increasingly ineffective until the organ dies. Benedicta's liver had swollen to adult size, distressing other organs not only through its failure but also through pressure. The failure of such an important organ sets off a chain reaction of other failures. Benedicta's kidneys could not operate properly, and her brain stem swelled down her spinal column. She also developed a staphylococcus infection.

What Dr. Kleinman found particularly unusual about Benedicta's case was that most children can be saved with the drug N-acetylcystein, "NAC." Typically, the organs of small children are unable to metabolize acetaminophen well, so if they are given NAC soon enough, the destructive process can be stopped. But though Benedicta was given NAC, as well as other drugs and treatment to reverse the condition, no one had known she had taken so much acetaminophen until days after the fact. Benedicta's metabolization of the drug had gone on for too long before its detection. As a result, the chain reaction of organ failure was in full progress.

The medical staff prepared Fr. McCarthy and his wife for the worst. He received a call from a doctor at 3:45 AM on Sunday, stating that his daughter had taken a bad turn.

Beside themselves, the McCarthys nevertheless agreed that Fr. McCarthy should fulfill an obligation to lead a two-day religious retreat on Christian nonviolence. While there, he was in constant contact with his wife by phone. He remembered being unable to watch a film shown to the retreatants—*Night and Fog*, a classic account of the Nazi persecution of the Jews at Auschwitz—because of the film's special impact. Not only had Edith Stein suffered the agonies of the gas depicted on the screen, but his two-year-old daughter was even then being destroyed by toxins. As the others watched the film, he went to a chapel and prayed.

According to Mrs. McCarthy's testimony, the first mention of invoking Benedicta's patron came during a telephone conversation Mrs. McCarthy had with her sister, Teresa Smit. Upon learning that the child was near death, Mrs. Smit, who also testified before the tribunal, suggested asking for the beatified nun's prayers. To the McCarthys the idea was natural and the plain course to take. Over the next few days, family members called friends and relatives—in Canada as well as the United States—asking them to invoke Edith Stein. They established a prayer chain. In addition, anyone who happened by the house, or called, was asked to pray in this fashion.

Then, on Sunday afternoon, after Benedicta had been placed at the head of the national list of liver transplant recipients, Mrs. McCarthy entered her daughter's room to pray. While including an acceptance of God's will for Benedicta, she laid her hands on the child's stomach and asked for healing through the intercession of Edith Stein. She recalled doing this several times.

The exact wording of Mrs. McCarthy's prayers was crucial to the miracle's authentication. It must be established that the Servant of God in question was invoked specifically. From the Vatican's perspective, as all graces are believed to come through Christ, prayers to Jesus do not call into question whether he permitted the healing to take place through the intercession of his servant. That, in fact, is how the Catholic Church envisions miracles happening: They are graces granted by God through the prayers of his servants, a cycle that underscores the connectedness of his church. However, had the McCarthys invoked other saints in their prayers—St. Francis of Assisi, for example—the Congregation of Saints would be unable to specifically attribute the miracle to the intercession of the servant in question.

From the McCarthys' perspective, there was little change in Benedicta's condition on Monday.

On Tuesday at 11:00 PM, however, Mrs. McCarthy was able to tell her husband that the situation did not seem to be worsening. The urgent need for the liver transplant was downgraded; doctors said that, considering the improvement, it would be better not to risk the operation just yet. Children Benedicta's age are as likely to die of such a radical operation as to survive it. Even if a transplant is a success, the body's rejection of the organ is a distinct possibility, and the recipient usually must take immunosuppressant drugs for life. Things seemed to be in a holding pattern, a lull that required careful scrutiny and attention.

Throughout the week, the prayer chain continued, invoking Edith Stein.

Medical records the following Monday, March 23, attest that the girl's condition was changing abruptly. Doctors' charts included statements that the child was "doing remarkably well." Mrs. McCarthy was told by a staff member that Benedicta's liver had somehow returned to normal size.

By Wednesday, the child was much better indeed and was coming out of her comatose state.

By Thursday or Friday, Benedicta was behaving like the same child the McCarthys had always known. From a medical perspective, Dr. Kleinman testified that over a period of days the girl's kidneys began to function, the liver shrank and regenerated, the herniated brain stem healed, and the girl's sensorium—her ability to think and function—cleared entirely. In order to monitor the drastic and perplexing change in Benedicta's condition, the staff kept her in the hospital for several more days. However, with no recurrence of any previously diagnosed problem, there was nothing left to do. The child was released.

Mrs. McCarthy stated that upon returning home, her daughter ran and played as normally as any other two-year-old. Of course, Benedicta was oblivious to the fact that only a week before, it had been the professional opinion of Massachusetts General Hospital that she would likely die.

Practically every potential miracle in modern times is a medical cure. And of those medical cures, certain cases do not qualify: for example, mental illness, cancer, and other diseases that can go into remission. The cure must not only be of a kind that does not remit, but it must also be durable. The cured must undergo medical examination, conducted by specialists independent of the Church and family, to verify that there is no trace of the disease or complication. In Benedicta McCarthy's case, two independent physicians examined the child. Six years after the cure, neither physician found anything that remotely indicated the multi-organ system failure that the girl had suffered.

In addition to gathering information from the family and medical testimony from the primary physician, Fr. Kieran and the other tribunal members gathered testimony from those in the prayer chain, the hospital staff, and consulting physicians. Signs were posted at Mass General asking that any staff member who had been involved with the case come forward. All medical records, X-rays, EKGs, blood tests, charts, lab documents, prescriptions, and appurtenant information—duly notarized—were amassed. When the tribunal closed in 1993, the *positio* in unbound form made its way to Rome by diplomatic courier.

As with any *positio* the McCarthy case also included testimony of those who were skeptical. All information, both favorable and unfavorable, is necessary for an objective decision. One physician, whom Dr. Kleinman had consulted by telephone during the case, was of the opinion that the cure was due to the NAC. Eventually, Dr. Kleinman had to go to Rome to explain this particular issue regarding the effectiveness of the drug. He was called to witness before the Congregation of Saints' medical consultants, the *Consulta Medica*.

According to Kenneth L. Woodward's work, *Making Saints*, the *Consulta* is a pool of around sixty physicians of all specialties. Members include medical school department heads, hospital directors, and others eminent in their fields. From this pool, a five-member panel is chosen to review each potential miracle. Two members of the panel are given a case; neither knows the other's identity. Both must pass judgment as either explicable by science or inexplicable by science. If both votes are negative, the case is rejected. If both are positive, or one is positive and one negative, the case is submitted to two other members of the panel, plus the *Consulta*'s president. Finally, the case is submitted to the full panel for vote.

In 1996, the Vatican flew Dr. Kleinman to Rome so that the *Consulta* could ask him more specific questions. From the *Consulta*'s perspective every aspect of a case must be reviewed: diagnosis, prognosis, adequacy of treatment, permanency of cure, and inexplicability. The panel, in what Dr. Kleinman has described as an argument, questioned him about the seriousness of Benedicta's illness and the effectiveness of the drugs. He had to convince them that Benedicta's condition would not have continued to worsen so drastically had she responded to the drugs, nor would her recovery have been so rapid. The meeting lasted for five hours. Finally, after withdrawing for deliberation, the group unanimously determined that the cure was inexplicable by science.

Even if the panel votes positively—which happens in fewer than half of the cases—the cure is not deemed miraculous by the *Consulta*. Their only job is to examine the events from a scientific standpoint; either the events can or cannot be explained. A positive vote simply means the cure will be submitted to the Congregation's theologians. This group must then determine that the invocation of the saint was proper and that the invocation was the cause of the cure. In the McCarthy case, the theologians found nothing objectionable. The event was approved as a miracle, and at the Consistory of Cardinals in May 1997, the pope announced that Teresia Benedicta of the Cross would be canonized a saint of the church.

Though the exact date of her canonization has not been set, it is likely the Pope's homily on that occasion will be similar to the one he delivered at Edith Stein's beatification in 1987, when he said:

> Today we greet in profound honor and holy joy a daughter of the Jewish people, rich in wisdom and courage, among these blessed men and women. . . . In going to die as one of her people, she enacted what she had once told her convent prioress: "It is not human activity that helps us—it is the suffering of Christ. To share in this is my desire." . . . She offered herself to God as a sacrifice for genuine peace . . . and above all, for her threatened and humiliated Jewish people. As Cardinal Hoffner has said: "Edith Stein is a gift, an invocation, and a promise for our time. May she be an intercessor with God for us and for our people and for all people."
>
> Blessed be Edith Stein, Sister Teresia Benedicta a Cruce, a true worshiper of God—in spirit and in truth. She is among the blessed. Amen.

The Church's process for authenticating miracles is supremely ironic—a long, bureaucratic, modern, earthly operation aimed at establishing something unearthly and inexplicable. The point of all this paper, notarization, testimony, deliberation, and debate is to be able to throw up one's hands and say that an event cannot be explained. The goal of the process is to be confounded. Surely this is the only such process of its type and scale in the world.

The McCarthys themselves were not involved with the case after the tribunal ended in 1993. They have not spoken to or met with Dr. Kleinman since their daughter was discharged from the hospital in 1987. As Benedicta has grown into adolescence, they have remained faithful to the cause of Edith Stein. As great a blessing as his daughter's healing has been for the family, Fr. McCarthy says, the miracle has less to do with the longevity of his daughter's life than it does with the mystery of God's purpose.

It is to the McCarthys' credit that they share their story. The average observer might consider the case peculiar at best, super-stitious at worst. To be misunderstood or disbelieved is, of course, a trial. Further, the McCarthys' surrender of their privacy must also be counted among their difficulties. Most would find both the inquiry and the considerable press attention unsettling and cumbersome. The *CBS Evening News*, the *Washington Post*, and countless magazines and periodicals, both religious and secular, have covered the story. People's scrutiny of the McCarthys is likely to continue for some time. Even at a private level, such things can be hard to think about, not only for those intimately involved with the case, but also for those who hear and accept its authen-ticity. For it admits of not only a belief in an infinite power, but also a belief that the infinite power is interested. Acutely. In us. In me. And comprehending that is nearly too much to bear.

Then again, it might be suggested, crosses are always hard to bear; but for those who do so triumphantly, heroically—as no one would doubt that Edith Stein did—they may perhaps win the great privilege of whispering kindnesses into the ear of God.

SIGHTINGS

RON
AUSTIN

BLUE SCREEN
MIRACLES AND MOVIES

EVERYTHING I KNOW ABOUT MIRACLES I learned from the movies.

What I know about miracles is that I cannot write about them without diminishing them. I can only write a screenplay that cannot be shot. What follows are fragmentary notes for the director.

I was born and raised in Hollywood, and all my beliefs and aspirations were shaped by the movies. I have worked for more than fifty years in an industry that calls itself "the business" and outsiders "civilians." These terms reveal a provinciality that supports its own belief system and entertains its own miracles. A movie miracle is real people doing real things in someone else's space and time. It is a miracle that is then sold in the marketplace.

A miracle cannot exist without our desire for it. The movie screen is, in fact, blank most of the time. Our vision wills the separate images into one, creating a reality greater than its parts. We know that what fills this space is illusory, yet we will its presence and it becomes real. The miraculous reveals itself despite our efforts to reject it. A miracle is more than its parts.

The fundamental miracle is not just that the world is, but that we are able to comprehend that it is, and that we can find it unbearably beautiful or terrifying. Miracles are instructive moments of joy or terror.

Miracles appear only in the real world. Miracles are not events subject to rational analysis, but they are profoundly anti-illusional. The ultimate revelation of the movies is that of their radical insufficiency—how reality escapes them. A good movie uses illusion for a glimpse of something that always lies beyond.

Movies give us analogies of miracles. Reality and appearance are always in conflict and a miracle does not resolve this tension; it reasserts it by pointing to a reality beyond what we know. A miracle is not an argument for a point of view but a reminder of the futility of argument. Miracles do not appear without faith and do not last without doubt.

The movie miracle begins when the lights come up.

Most movies should be seen on airplanes. It is the perfect environment. You can eat and drink, and you are going someplace at the same time.

I am flying home at thirty thousand feet when I become aware that someone is in trouble. I look up. A volcano has erupted halfway through dinner. I am quietly reading Robert Hass and people are fleeing from a fiery volcanic flow on twelve separate screens. Only a miracle can save them. The clouds outside my window, hugely white and once cavorting like dolphins, are now slowly diminishing. I stare at them. Are they real?

Later, I have almost forgotten about the movie. Someone is dying as coffee is served. A teenage voice from the seat behind groans to his companion, "It's lame," but they keep on their headsets. I do not know who dies or why. The miracle on the twelve screens has come and gone. I look out. The clouds are now distant strangers. We put on our seat belts. Somewhere below in Sonora a Yaqui Indian lights a fire with Diamond matches.

Tonight there will be TV in the cantina.

My window is opaque. It has become a reflection of my mental haze. It has become my "blue screen." The blue screen is a movie process in which actors are filmed against a screen, and other backgrounds are later superimposed. We all have our own inner blue screens.

I always have had an intricate interior life which I converted from a neurotic condition into a profession. Writing was a compulsion redeemed. I was shaped by fiction, the work of writers, so I became a writer. But I eventually discovered that all bad writing is a form of cowardice. So, not being sufficiently brave, I became a producer.

Good writing shocks us into believing what we would not dare otherwise believe: that reality is gracious. This continues to point toward miracles.

There are miraculous people in movies. Hollywood's best movies were often miracles of personality. Movie stars became our cultural saints, their transparency allowing us to see into ourselves. Many of them still last today as stars, that is, "astrological signs" of our desires. The stars of my time, Charlie Chaplin and Buster Keaton, Fred Astaire and Gene Kelly, all entered my real world.

To be in their actual presence, to observe their foibles, their vanities and insecurities, did not demystify their status but somehow enhanced it. They became flesh and blood to me as I watched them strain at their craft, yet they remain icons. No one believes in the mythology of Hollywood more than its practitioners.

Movies are created in Hollywood by a process which, if logical, efficient, and harmonious, assures that the movie will be bad. Good movies are created by the internal conflicts that provoke and require a subversive counter-process of transcendence. No one understands what this means. No one knows how it is done, especially the people who succeed at it. *Citizen Kane* is the great American film because of the manner in which it was made. The studio thought it was a screen test. A good script is one that deceives the front office into thinking they know why they are making it. A good writer is a practitioner of the virtue of deceit.

There are only two things to make movies about: the tragedy of life, and the discovery of hope. Movies are about sex and violence because we are afraid to address the obscenities in intimacy and death. Love stories are all the same: We never love each other as much as we should, and we are never loved as much as we need.

We learn to make love from the movies. (We used to learn to make love *in* the movies.) But most movies are teachers that skip every other chapter and always the last one. Beware: The more realistic in detail a movie is, especially with sex, the deeper the illusion.

Hollywood makes dreams that money can buy, which is to say, love is for sale. The process kills the art just as the feigning of pleasure kills love. This is why the only untroubled conscience in Hollywood is that of the thief.

I have spent fifty years working in Hollywood, and I do not know what a good movie is. What I have learned is what a good movie is not. (I am consoled to know that this is good theology: Via negativa.) I know how movies are made, especially bad ones. No one knows how good movies are made. This also is the subject of miracles.

I know that good movies please and disturb us, and bad movies excite us into sleep. The test of a good movie (we still do not know what it is) is the peace and joy that lie at the far side of our incomprehension and agitation. Bad movies can satisfy us but good movies set us free.

This brings us back to miracles.

On my blue screen there is now a darkened bedroom. A troubled, middle-aged dreamer comes awake at night.

My dream of the crucifixion brings me awake, wet with sweat. It absorbs all the horror and cruelty that I have seen in life. Somewhere within the dream the man Jesus looks at me with eyes that express something beyond my comprehension and that I understand in the deepest part of me. I will later dream the same dream as if it is not mine.

As a merchandiser of fiction, I know that the imagination has incredible powers. But this suffering Christ conforms to that of the ages. I realize that I am a very ordinary person. All of my subjective experiences gather me into a fold of time.

I remember also one day in my hillside garden because of its ordinariness. I felt rather than heard a music within and without me, both in the heavens and beneath the earth. I did not speak to anyone about this. I never thought of it as a miracle.

All of this leads to the miracle of belief.

My blue screen is now the interior of a church. A man hides in the last row. He stands in confusion when others kneel, kneels when they sit. I am that man.

People have asked what my religion was before I became a Christian, and I tell them that it was "show business." It is almost true. The idealism of the Hollywood of my youth was largely political, strictly left-wing. History was the source of hope. There was also, of course, the god of hedonism, but this devotion was exaggerated. Movie people get up very early in the morning.

Our old gods of politics and sex railed and died. Self-reverential art became commerce. The avant-garde became a prerequisite undergraduate course. Sex became dangerous or, worse, predictable. Our attempt to replace God with human history failed. My Hollywood became a mausoleum of ideals.

But the truth is, I don't know why I became a Christian.

I had slowly constructed my own structure of belief out of what I thought was unique material, my own confused life, only to find that I had built a small and still incomplete chapel. All that was missing was the cross.

I remember attending my first mass, anonymous in the last row, and losing my voice in emotion when addressing "you, my brothers and sisters," in confession. I was suddenly united to other human beings by my frailty. I never thought of this as a miracle.

I worship and believe as a Catholic because Catholics believe in truth even if it eludes them, or perhaps *because* it eludes them. I believe in the dogmas of the Church, or, at least, I think I do. Dogma has a bad name. I think dogmatic assertions are the rules of the game of love as they are in marriage. Speculate excessively and you risk the relationship. For me, the opposite of dogmatic is systematic. I know this is probably not very good theology, but perhaps we can we agree on this much: Possibly there are no certain truths, but there are certainly lies.

So I became a Christian to find out why I became a Christian. Just in time.

My blue screen is once again a darkened bedroom. Now it is the grieving lover who stands alone at the window. God is at the door. (We do not need special effects, please.) I am the lover and the one I loved has died. Death is still in the room; it is filling my being. I open the curtain and the garden outside the window is full of sunlight. The words within me, free and spontaneous, bursting through my grief, are those of gratitude. (Are they my words?)

There are no words to describe this miracle. The words are the miracle.

My blue screen is now the endless ocean. Facing it is a man who thinks he is alone. I think I am alone. But God greets me one day on the wharf at Santa Barbara. He cracks jokes. We laugh together. Sometime later I drive to the cemetery above the sea. No one I know is buried there. I am a grave tourist. I sit on a stone bench among the dead, and, calling upon St. Teresa's "mad girl," I summon all of me, past and future, dead and alive and yet to die. My mother places a bassinet at one end of the gathering and my cries can be heard coming from it. Next sits the wondering six-year-old, and, coming closer, the self-conscious youth, the challenging adolescent, the young father, the successful fool, and, closest, the grieving lover. Beyond, in the other direction, extending into a dark infinity, all the dead rise to join me, strangers and friends. And we sit in calm quiet and watch the ocean.

The turning point for many of us is an experience of something dying in such a way that it creates something living and continuous. Yet I never thought of this as a miracle.

There is the blue screen of the computer as the writer writes, backspaces, and deletes.

Miracles do not need our defense. God has given us miracles and it is our problem to live with them. We may not welcome them, but I do not think we should try to talk about God behind his back.

I believe, but I confess that I am impatient. I have discovered that I would rather ask questions endlessly than wait for God's response. I want to know the eternal God, and yet I cannot even begin to plumb the depths of my own consciousness. Even when I pray, the question remains: Who gets the first word, God or me? So I swim each day through my own emptiness. It is my spiritual sea. I fear abandonment, as I fear drowning, but abandonment is exactly what I need and seek.

The "great choice" is God or me. I am not given the choice of nothingness or absurdity. These are both evasions. Nor is the choice mere rationality, itself another evasion. The hardest choice is between the high discipline of aloneness, the desert, or the miseries of community. All the rest is commentary.

But I do not want to be a village explainer. I do not want to argue. I have no quarrel with anyone more than myself. If I'm arguing, then I'm too busy for God. I want to know my sins, because, whatever they cost me, they may be all that I have to offer.

These fragmented thoughts about movies may appear to be aphorisms about the miraculous nature of belief, but they are only drama. The blessed are those deprived of aphorisms. They who are left without any recourse. This leads us to the subject of miracles.

The blue screen is blank. No more movies except in memory.

The son taking the father's hand in *Bicycle Thieves,* and the dog returning to the old man in *Umberto D.*

The poor flying to heaven in *Miracle in Milan,* and the Count playing the music machine in *Rules of the Game.*

The old man on the swing at night in *Ikiru,* and the old man remembering the picnic in *Wild Strawberries.*

Trevor Howard and Celia Johnson's parting looks in *Brief Encounter,* and the couple recognizing each other in *A Day in the Country.*

Zampano groaning at the end of *La Strada,* and Marcello calling to the young girl in *La Dolce Vita.*

The two escapes: *A Man Condemned to Death* and *A Nous la Liberté.*

Fonda's stately dancing in *My Darling Clementine,* and Guinness's proud, staggering walk in *Bridge on the River Kwai.*

The flop sweat of Olivier's "Archie Rice," and Brando's death in the garden in *The Godfather.*

François, frozen in fear at the end of *400 Blows,* and Charlie Chaplin's smile at the end of *City Lights.*

Everything I know about miracles I learned from the movies.

ERIN MCGRAW

THE WAY OF IMPERFECTION
THE UNEXPECTED TERESA OF AVILA

I send you this hair shirt. . . .
It can be worn on any part of
the body and put on in any
way so long as it feels
uncomfortable. . . . It makes
me laugh to think how you
send me sweets and pre-
sents and money, and I send
you hair shirts.

—Teresa of Avila,
to her brother [1]

54

I MET SANCTITY FACE TO FACE WHEN I WAS IN SECOND GRADE, preparing with the other children in my class to make my first communion. Communion, solemn and thrilling, required a full year of preparation—in geography we colored maps of the Holy Land, and in reading Sister led us through tales of faithful little boys and girls who gave up their hopes for roller skates so that other children could have warm clothes. In arithmetic we grappled with problems worded in apposite terms: "If Billy eats a piece of toast at 7:00 and then has to fast for an hour, what time will he be able to receive communion?"

For months, every aspect of our lives was canted toward the great event, and my excitement swelled like a bubble. Holiness would soon be granted to me, placed on my tongue like a present. Once that present had been given, all I had to do was choose not to sin, and I could be a saint. Half sick with importance and anticipation, I went around counting the remaining days, fretful that untimely death might make me miss my chance to go to heaven and shower blessings on my friends and family.

Into this supercharged air of holy ambition, a new girl joined our class. A plump, dough-faced child who held her hands clutched before her as if she were squeezing something between them, her name was Regina Mary, and her family had moved to southern California from all the way across the country. Sister was counting on us, this year in particular, to extend a friendly hand to her. After she introduced Regina Mary, Sister paused a moment, then added, "I hope you will remember how to be examples for one another."

We all understood the delicate chiding behind Sister's admonition, so at recess Regina Mary was the first girl chosen for dodgeball, although her serene face and thick, bruised legs did not make her look like much of an athlete. Sure enough, she was the first girl out; she didn't move, even a step, when the ball came whistling toward her and caught her on the thigh. A few minutes later, when I was out too, I said to her, "Too bad you got out so fast. It wasn't fair."

"I know," she said. "I'm offering it up." She smiled at me, and brushed her fingers over the spot the ball had smacked. Unsure what to say, I strolled back to the sidelines where other girls were noisily cheering. Regina Mary stayed where she was, alone, her hands once again clamped before her, and I suddenly realized she was, right in front of everybody, offering to Jesus her humiliation and new bruise for his greater glory. I was glad I had already tried to talk to her, so I wouldn't have to extend a friendly hand again.

Back in the classroom, Sister told us to open our battered blue religion books. I snuck a glance at Regina Mary, who wore an idle, nonspecific smile, and I wondered whether she had already memorized the book. Probably.

"Why did God make man?" Sister asked, the first of the Baltimore Catechism questions we were supposed to have learned a month before. Twenty-five pairs of eyes stared at our desk tops. We were bad on the Baltimore Catechism. Sister let the silence stretch and tremble before she did what I knew she was going to do, to set an example. "Regina Mary?" she asked.

"Man is made to know, love, and serve God." Regina Mary's voice was richly confident, and Sister smiled. At that moment, the puzzled discomfort I had felt on the playground took root, and I hated Regina Mary.

Several of the other girls were already working out mincing imitations of her, which after a week of practice and critique became mean, precise, and funny. I didn't always join them when they copied her walk, spine pencil-straight and folded hands carried level with her nose, but when I had the chance I kicked the dodgeball straight at her, then watched her drift off the field with an unmistakable air of relief.

At home, away from her, guilt lapped over me; holiness required that I love Regina Mary, and on my knees before bed I could sometimes work up a watery admiration for her good study habits. One day, after an especially guilty night when I feared that saintliness was sliding away from me like a tide, I forced myself to walk over to where she was sitting alone, eating her sandwich. "You don't have to sit by yourself," I said. "There's room for you." I gestured toward the picnic table where the rest of the girls were sitting together, noisily sharing Fritos and all but incapacitated with giggles over Maureen Connor, who said she liked Ringo best. Regina Mary politely smiled and rested her sluggish hand on my arm, a gesture borrowed from the sisters. My small pool of admiration began evaporating.

"I have a Friend for lunch," Regina Mary said. "I do not want him to sit alone."

I was frustrated that when I went back to join my friends, I felt more in the wrong than ever—a feeling I built on by shouting, "Guess what Regina Mary just said!" Later, when I overheard Sister telling my mother that Regina Mary was a saint among us, I gloomily supposed she was right. By then it was clear to me that I was not cut out of saint fabric, and I gave up my efforts at prayer and fell in love, as girls my age did, with horses.

For the next twenty-three years I assumed that I disliked saints, and I was never proved wrong. Every saintly personality I met had some distillation of Regina Mary's fat self-satisfaction, and the saints I read about frequently had alarming, not to say disgusting, habits: the practice of one of the Saint Simons, for instance, of tying a dead dog to his belt to remind him of the corruptibility of the flesh. Saints might be inscrutably good for the earth and necessary to the cosmos, but they were troublesome companions; a person needed to be a saint in order to put up with one.

By the time I turned thirty, though, I found myself less certain about my judgments and less choicy about companions. My life had entered a dark stretch—career at a frightening standstill, marriage in shreds. Feeling trapped and despairing, I started to read self-help books, but I could not stand the chirpy uplift most of them provided. Life was hard, and I wanted to find a book that acknowledged that fact before it rushed on to rebirth and renewal and all the happy stuff. The desire to contemplate suffering, of course, brought me back to the classics of spirituality, some of which I had studied. I considered Augustine, the Little Flower, the desert fathers. In the end I chose the *Life* of Teresa of Avila—Teresa of Jesus, as she called herself—because it seemed to me that anyone who lived through Inquisition Spain would know how to give full measure to human pain.

In my beaten-down state, I was ready for stern lectures and exhortations. If necessary, I was ready to be reminded to offer up my trials to God. What I was in no way ready for was the first sentence of the *Life*, which I read one exhausted evening after work: "If I had not been so wicked it would have been a help to me that I had parents who were virtuous and feared God, and also that the Lord granted me his favor to make me good."[2]

Startled, I reread the sentence. I knew all about saints who tediously protested their unworthiness, and who explained at extreme length how their salvation was due to the good examples and intercession of others. But I had never run across a saint who was pithy and funny. I will not say that the way before me suddenly looked bright, but at least it looked more interesting than I had expected, and I began to think I had a companion for the journey.

Most people, if they know a single thing about Teresa, know about Bernini's gorgeous, baroque, wholly excessive sculpture of the saint in ecstasy. The Teresa the sculptor depicts is young, wild, beautiful, and her face and body are twisted in a passion that is clearly orgasmic. Bernini took as inspiration the most notorious passage from the *Life*, in which Teresa describes one of her visions. An angel, she writes, appears before her.

> In his hands I saw a long golden spear and at the end of the iron tip I seemed to see a point of fire. With this he seemed to pierce my heart several times so that it penetrated to my entrails. When he drew it out, I thought he was drawing them out with it and he left me completely afire with a great love for God. The pain was so sharp that it made me utter several moans; and so excessive was the sweetness caused me by this intense pain that one can never wish to lose it. . . .[3]

Not surprisingly, Freudian scholars have had a field day with this passage. They see in it a banner example of repressed sexuality taking the guise of religious rapture—an interpretation I see myself, as I imagine any twentieth-century reader can. But the Freudian interpretation is not absolute. To dismiss Teresa's description of her vision, calling it merely the delusion of a sex-starved woman, strikes me as simplistic and vulgar, and it does not take sufficiently into account the facts of Teresa's life.

For one thing, such an interpretation overlooks the likelihood that Teresa was aware of the freighted nature of her language. The golden spear with its iron tip, the pain she wishes never to end—to assume that Teresa could not hear the charged overtones of her words is to assume that she was stupidly naive and had never read a romantic novel or heard a flirtatious conversation, although the *Life* makes clear she had done plenty of both. And such an assumption does not ponder the end of the paragraph, where Teresa says tartly, "So sweet are the colloquies of love which pass between the soul and God that if anyone thinks I am lying I beseech God, in his goodness, to give him the same experience." You think I'm a hysterical woman? the sentence implies. *You* try writing about an angel's visit.

The descent from rapture to a tone very close to annoyance is almost comical, and refreshing. Rarely does Teresa get caught up for long in the sort of fervent exultation that characterizes the writings of many other saints, exultation that is apparently such a delight to write and that is so trying to read. Teresa's paragraphs of praise and her protests of her own unworthiness sit squarely beside more earthbound passages, in which she points out that she has work to do or reminds her nuns to quit grousing. In the juxtaposition between joyful, holy gratitude and practical concerns I glimpse a real life, one I can imagine trying to imitate, in which the moutaintop experiences are very, very reliably accompanied by descents back to the valley. As one of her nuns was reported to have said, "Blessed be God who has given us a Saint that we can imitate!"[4]

I cannot, of course. I do not have a tenth of Teresa's passion for God, and God alone, and I do not yearn to shut myself off from the world in order better to pray. But a reader—me—is able to feel, however inappropriately, that Teresa is imitable because her writing makes sanctity feel close, possible, a friendly option. Teresa's holiness did not remove her from the world, but plunged her into it, face first. Never do I have the sense that her immersion in God and the raptures she describes exempted her from the small, daily irritations that constantly encircle me. God sent to her annoyances as well as delights, and she wrote about them all.

Describing the ecstatic states that descended over her in prayer, she complains, "they do not even help one to pray better." Wearily pondering some of the timid confessors that surrounded her, she comments, "I am more afraid of people who fear the devil than I am of the devil himself." [5] Delicately correcting one of those confessors on a matter of theology, she writes, "What a strange kind of belief is this, that, when God has willed that a toad should fly, he should wait for it to do so by its own efforts"—and then, a paragraph later, "whenever we think of Christ, we should remember with what love he has bestowed all these favors upon us . . . for love begets love." [6]

Some commentators, particularly Teresa's contemporaries, dismissed her ability to blend worldly and heavenly concerns as self-contradictory and symptomatic of an undisciplined mind. But I take comfort from her ability to hold joy and exasperation in a balanced tension. From Teresa's perspective, all things are in God, including inept confessors, haughty, troublesome nuns, and toadlike humanity. Rather than trying to rise above the frustrations that besiege her, she gives vent to her exasperation, asking God to free her from nuns with mystical pretensions and priests of only a little learning. And although she often prays for patience, it is clear that she does not believe her impatience separates her from the God she loves. If anything, she works up gratitude for the impatience, seeing it as one small, humble way to follow her humble Lord.

"I deserve nothing but crosses, and so I praise him who is always giving them to me," she says with typical wryness of tone. [7] Holy suffering was central to sixteenth-century Castilian devotion, and bloody, crippling mortifications were common for both religious and laypeople. In the context of the prevailing attitudes, Teresa's approach to bodily mortification was restrained: When she founded her first convent, she took with her only a single haircloth with iron links.[8] Some years later, writing her rule for the reformed Carmelites, she specified that birch twigs, never leather, were to be used for bodily penance.[9] In her view, there is scarce need for us to inflict pain on ourselves. God can be counted on to send the mortification we need, and Teresa begs her nuns to be as willing to accept tiny trials of vanity and the spirit with the same zeal they might be willing to take up the leather cord.

This advice displays shrewd insight that must have been maddening to certain of her more dramatically inclined nuns. Teresa understood the prideful joy of self-inflicted martyrdom, and she also understood how easily a person can lose track of God-centered devotion under the peculiar ecstasy of deprivation. Having been, as she would say, so wicked herself, she knew the many tricks and shams of apparent holiness, knew how a sister might take on extra mortifications in order to gain a reputation for holiness, or might appear rapt in prayer in order to avoid dishwashing. But the Lord, Teresa famously pointed out, walks among the pots and pans.[10] If she valued a single virtue above all others, that virtue was humility, accepting gratefully whatever trials God sees fit to give.

Teresa knew better than most just how imaginative God could be in the creation of trials. She had a slow start as a saint, spending close to twenty years in the convent practicing indifferent prayer and highly imperfect observance of her vow of obedience. But once her spirit caught fire, she craved above all things to dwell in uninterrupted, silent, personal love for her Lord. Unfortunately for her, she was already receiving the divine favors that would make her one of the most famous, visited, and busy women of her age.

"O my Lord, how true it is that as soon as a person renders thee some service, he is rewarded with great trials!" she wrote in

the *Book of the Foundations*.[11] Only a few years after she founded her first convent, St. Joseph's in Avila, much of Castile was
talking about the prioress who so frequently levitated during
prayer that she entreated her nuns to kneel on her habit, pinning
her to the floor. She became a celebrity: Pilgrims and suppli-
cants came to her, begging through the grille that was supposed
to separate her from the world, that she pray for them and teach
them how to pray. Even more troubling to church authorities
were the rumors that she conversed directly with Jesus in her
prayers and counseled her nuns to do the same, a dangerously
Lutheran practice. For the rest of her life Teresa would be forced
to prove, again and again, her orthodoxy, writing the books that
became classics of contemplative theology.

She enjoyed only four years of true enclosure before she was
ordered, by superiors who had their own quarrels inside the
Church, to travel and found other convents—ultimately seventeen in all, plus two monasteries. This supposedly enclosed nun
spent over fifteen years in near-constant travel, with its attendant
planning, wrangling, and finagling. As she struggled against hostile church and civic authorities, she drew on reserves of personal charm that we are told by her contemporaries were extraordinary, and she drove her delicate health, several times, to collapse. It is no wonder, she wrote grimly during one of her peri-
ods of recuperation, that God has so few friends, considering the
way he treats the ones he has.

The contradictions in Teresa's life spread and branch like
cracks in ice. The prioress who distrusted raptures, recom-
mending that nuns who underwent ecstatic states be given extra
kitchen duty, was frequently immobilized by trances and visions
of her Savior. The mystic who was embarrassed by her visions

was ordered by her superiors to write books about them. The woman who yearned to withdraw from the world was forced to travel all over Spain. The nun who fled her first, social, gossipy convent in order to found a house of silence and prayer had to rely on her abilities to charm men into giving her land and buildings for new convents. The mishmash of intention and actuality is hardly what we expect of a life devoted to God.

For this reason—that the firmer she grew in personal devotion, the more secular her life became—pondering Teresa's story never fails to cheer me up. Any believer who has struggled with a God who pulls us away from our presumptive notions of holiness, who nudges us into endeavors we had hoped to avoid and arenas where we had never meant to go, will recognize the powerful irony of Teresa's situation. Those readers understand her belief that we should take God very seriously and ourselves not seriously at all. While funny, this belief is no joke.

And seriousness, of course, not jokes, is what most of us expect from a life devoted to God. Contemplating seriousness brings me back to Regina Mary, that humorless child. No joke: Sometimes I think, in frustration, that her example influenced me more than any other religious teaching I ever had. Although Regina Mary herself managed to break free from her claustrophobic holiness—I heard that she became pregnant when she was fifteen, a rumor that afforded me years of sour satisfaction—I carry her pious little example with me still. It does not take much for me to start primly lecturing myself or, God help me, others about how our sufferings are as nothing compared to those of him who died for us.

While Teresa would certainly agree with the sentiment, she would be quick to point out that no one needs to add to the general load. She loved a cheerful spirit, not a sanctimonious one, and had little patience for the sort of piety that moons around and assures everyone in earshot that it hardly even notices its trials. In humble acceptance of trials, she says again and again, is holiness found. And I believe her, because she had some mighty trials. Most of her convents were founded despite considerable opposition, both civic and ecclesiastical. Not uncommonly did Teresa find herself sneaking a wagonload of nuns into town at night, only to discover in the morning that the building she had been pledged was in the market section of town or was missing walls. Once a rainstorm forced her nuns to huddle outside the city walls for a night—a providential delay, since the next morning bulls were run through the streets. On another occasion Teresa posted a guard near her new convent's makeshift tabernacle, then stole downstairs several times during the night to make sure no local force, opposed to the new nuns, crept in to steal the chalice containing the blessed hosts. Is this the work of God? complained one of her nuns, dismayed to find that her new convent had holes in the external walls that she could fit her fist through. It is *all* God's work, Teresa assured her, and every irritant is a paving stone in the path to perfection.

Perfection! She uses the word often and confidently, reminding her readers that they should want to attain nothing less, trying to convince them that the state is within their grasp. For myself, I am not convinced. Distracted and frustrated by meetings, money, the smallness of most of my efforts, and the manifest lack of holiness in my life, I find the idea of perfection dismaying—a reaction that is just one of the ways, I suppose, I can see that I am not a saint. Nevertheless, I take heart in Teresa's exhortations, her reassurance that small crosses are crosses indeed, content that I am walking a right path, however little progress I make.

I don't believe that I exaggerate much when I say a thousand times, though it may start a quarrel with the one who ordered me to play down the account of my sins—and mightily prettified it is all coming out! I beg him for the love of God to cut out nothing about my sins, for it is just there that the glory of God is shown—by what he will put up with in a human soul.[12]

Teresa is generally remembered in conjunction with St. Joseph, to whom she had a respectful devotion and dedicated her first convent. But the saints she truly loved were the transgressors, the headline sinners who discovered God in the heart of their own sinfulness—Augustine and Magdalene. She found in them what she yearned to find among the saints: not martyrdom or miracles, but plain human souls, flawed as she perceived her own to be flawed, redeemed by the love of an astonishingly tolerant God.

Augustine and Magdalene scare me; they are too distant, too lofty, too wholly holy. I cannot imagine their worrying about getting the grocery shopping done. I need a saint who feels cut closer to human scale, an example whose own life was a patchwork of chores and frustrations. And I need a saint who reminds me that genuine holiness has little to do with pat piety or a preconceived notion of sanctity. So I ponder Teresa, who rejoiced when she found her Lord in everyday chores, who relished irony, and who recognized her God in the contrary movements of his will.

NOTES

1 Jill Haak Adels, *The Wisdom of the Saints* (New York:
Oxford University Press, 1987), 171.

2 *The Complete Works of St. Teresa of Avila*, trans. and ed. E. Allison Peers
(London: Sheed and Ward, 1946), I:10.

3 Ibid., 192–193.

4 Henri Joly, *Saint Teresa*, translated by Emily M. Waller
(London: Duckworth & Co., 1903), 156.

5 Victoria Lincoln, *Teresa—A Woman* (Albany, NY: State
University of New York Press, 1985), xl, 55.

6 *Complete Works*, III: 142–143.

7 Francis L. Gross, with Toni Perior Gross, *The Making of a
Mystic: Seasons in the Life of Teresa of Avila*, (Albany, NY: State
University of New York Press, 1993), 69.

8 Joly, *Saint Teresa*, 147.

9 Lincoln, *Teresa*, 96.

10 *Complete Works*, III: 22.

11 Ibid., 192.

12 Lincoln, *Teresa*, 29.

DAVID BOROFKA

UNDERLAND

ONE WEEKEND A MONTH, my wife goes away. She attends a course on the analysis of dreams, those latent symbols that, if Freud and Jung are to be believed, reveal ourselves to ourselves. The class is held in the hills overlooking Santa Barbara; when she leaves our home in the Central Valley, she drives through poor towns that have spent the past decades specializing in the refuse of agriculture—junkyards and the rusting hulks of forgotten and archaic equipment. In dry seasons, dust drifts across the highway. Eventually, however, the dispiriting trash of the rural is replaced by vineyards and orchards, which are in turn replaced by the golden hills of Paso Robles, and the coastline of San Luis Obispo, and the Mediterranean paradise of Santa Barbara itself. It is a journey of contrasts—either/or—that she makes, and it is preparation for the class itself, in its respect for the permeable membranes that divide our conscious from our unconscious selves. She comes home each month with stories of visions and visitations: a hawk sailing over the highway, a flock of cranes in a marsh, the transcendent image she received one night of an orca rising above all our heads.

In the meantime, I fumble as best I can as father and home-owner; the grass needs to be mowed, my younger daughter needs her hair brushed, the television burbles Saturday morning cartoons. These are my visitations, my transcendental moments. It is precious time, usually, but not so this morning. Something lingers in the air, some weight or dark cloud that will not leave. I feel assaulted, threatened even by ordinary things: the sections of newspaper scattered like autumn leaves across the dining room table, the dishabille of the beds, the indolence of our newest cat lying in a spot of sun, my older daughter, her cheek creased by pillow and blanket, fuddle-headed with sleep, squint-ing into the morning light. Innocent pictures by themselves, but viewed through the lens of this nameless dread, they become the images of burden and oppression. A request for orange juice becomes a death march into the kitchen. Washing the dirty dishes is more than I can bear. A question becomes an inquisition. I snap at my daughters, turn up the volume on the television, and cover my head with my hands.

Later, having showered and dressed, I decide that such emo-tional sensations are the product of weakness, a temperament sensitized to the nuances of my wife's absence. Errands must be run—the bank, the grocery store, the dry cleaner. The everyday waits for no one's crisis of will; moving forward is the antidote to the doldrums.

We pile into the car, but the foreboding does not loosen its grip. My daughters fuss in the back seat while I stare into the glare of a harsh April morning. Walking across the parking lot to the grocery store, pushing an empty cart, I nearly fall to my knees, crippled by the sense not so much that my life is coming apart as it is vaporizing atom by atom. My daughters' chatter, echoing as though in an empty room, is wasted upon a nonperson, a nothing in shoes. I am losing even the capacity for irritation. No surface has depth, no idea has substance, and I am prey to the thought that this is as it has always been. In the back seat, trapped in the rearview mirror, the girls lapse into silence; with the intuition of children they have realized that all is not right in the front seat and have fallen into a dependence on one another. Somehow we accomplish our list of things to do, travel home, put away our purchases, and stare into the maw of eight remaining daylight hours. My older daughter wants to read me a poem, the younger wants me to watch a tape, but I beg them both to leave me alone, alone, alone. I love my children, but right now I cannot stand to hear their voices. Like Wordsworth I yearn for "those shadowy recollections" of the divine and immortal, but the only voice that resonates for me is the plaintive bleating of Matthew Arnold: ". . . neither joy, nor love, nor light, / Nor certitude, nor peace, nor help for pain. . . ."

Everywhere I look, it seems, I am ensnared by such dualities—Santa Barbara and Fresno, dream and experience, transcendence and depression—and I am trapped on the "wrong" side of either/or.

In *Darkness Visible*, his memoir on depression, William Styron noted the difficulty, even for the artist, in describing the malady's torment for those unafflicted. The best metaphor of the illness, he writes, is Dante's, the opening lines of *Inferno*: "In the middle of the journey of our life / I found myself in a dark wood / For I had lost the right path." The journey of our life. For the reader, bells go off, whistles shriek: metaphor a-comin'. Nothing new here. In most contemporary literature, however, transcendent moments are generally reserved for some sort of Joycean epiphany, couched metaphorically in the language of ordinary things. But Dante is different in Styron's reading, for here the supernatural, a man's descent into hell, is treated as the literal activity, while the language, by its suggestion, entices us to see this apparent spiritual journey as a metaphor for the everyday.

I have been thinking about such boundaries quite a bit lately, prompted in no small measure by my brief glimpse into that darkness, and in retrospect, I can trace my dilemma of that weekend to a similar inversion: the events in Rancho Santa Fe that headlined the news throughout that week and the emotional chords that thrummed as a result. The suicides of the Heaven's Gate cult reawakened certain dormant impulses within myself: a yearning to know what is quite possibly unknowable and a certainty, bordering on arrogance, that one already knows it, driving the otherwise rational mind to acts that, according to an objective or simply indifferent outsider, seem desperate and horribly misguided.

There was something of the literalizing impulse behind their suicides, it seems, some refusal to welcome or tolerate metaphor. Instead of seeing in Hale-Bopp an emblem of the divine, they saw in its shadow a spaceship, come to take them home. Metaphor literalized in a manner worthy of Gabriel Garcia Marquez's peasants, their literal journey, as in Dante, had a supernatural itinerary. But instead of a celestial destination, they arrived in yesterday's headlines, a cautionary tale: Don't believe everything you hear.

There was a quality of group-think unbearable to us on the other side of Heaven's Gate, some sort of mass hysteria, at once inexplicable, wrong-headed, and unfair, reminding us once again of the fragility and frailty of groups, whether in Waco or Jonestown, Oneida or Bethel or the Kingdom as proclaimed by Matthias. Each community obeyed the teachings of a charismatic figure; they heard a siren call inaudible to outsiders—to those chained in the dark of an earthen cave—and they declared it fit only for the ears of other true believers such as themselves. But lest those of us watching the news on television be too smug—having escaped the fate of Marshall Applewhite's disciples, or those of David Koresh, John Humphrey Noyes, or Wilhelm Kiel—we are reminded of Jesus' words to his own: "He who has ears to hear, let him hear." Who has missed the boat? Then again, how does one know whether a boat—or a spaceship, for that matter—exists in the first place? The Kingdom of heaven, we are told, resides within a community of hearts of those who believe, and yet is it not disturbing to think that such faith might be nothing more than a communal dream: a wish reinforced by others of similar desires?

I know something of groups. For seven years I was part of such a community, an extended family that wielded tremendous influence over the behavior of its members. In this hothouse of religious fervor, Jesus may have been Lord, but the interpersonal dynamic of the group was Master. Individual decisions regarding career or education were offered up for collective debate, members offered to the community at large their most personal confessions, and it was expected that all parts of all lives were open for inspection. We were a large family living in a small house with all the injuries and insult attendant to a lack of privacy.

There were bound to be gaffes, of course, produced by ignorance, denial, or naivete: depression and eating disorders treated solely as though they were crises of the spirit; past incidents of

incest and rape that were thought to be resolved through forgiveness alone. (We were hardly original, of course; at the community of Oneida, it was believed that mutual criticism and confession were responsible for the cure of anything from earaches
to diphtheria.) And yet as misguided as such formulaic, too-
simple analyses might have been, a certain comfort was derived
by the intimacy—in knowing as well as being known.

More insidious, perhaps in retrospect, was my own loss of
appreciation for the subtle hints, the whispered intimations of
God. More consumed with hermeneutics than with aesthetics, I
mocked the Pharisees as I surely became one. It became terribly
important to know whether or not Scripture could be interpreted
analogously or allegorically, whether or not the arguments for a
second Isaiah or the book of Q were sound, whether one were
pre-, post-, or a-millennial.

Hair-splitting, as any lawyer will tell you, is quite tiring (not to
mention tiresome to those in the immediate vicinity). It is even
more so when undertaken by well-meaning amateurs. In my own
case, the net effect of such catechistic wrangling was the eleva-
tion of the abstract and a diminishment in importance of the
emotional and sensory: of soulful, ineffable, and private experience. My abstraction took the form of an arbitrary and sporadic
asceticism. Now and again I fasted, and once I deprived myself
of sleep on the grounds that it was time wasted, a belief that lasted only until I nearly fell from a roof.

Yet, as religious as I was and we were, I can remember feeling
only that some essential experience, a feeling of spirituality, was
being denied me. Frankly, aside from those universally defining
moments such as a first kiss or the sight of one's newborn child,
I have enjoyed moments of more metaphysical consequence
while engaged in some sweaty activity: the feeling of connection
when a forehand drive in racquetball comes back a rollout, or

better still, a magical moment during a high school tackling drill, when I put the top of my helmet into our fullback's chest, felt my back bow and my hips drive forward. I stood him up, then drove him onto his back: an instant of crystal clarity and grace that never occurred in quite the same magical way during the chaos and ambiguity of an actual game.

Less magical is the memory of several years later when my yearning for some such experience in a religious context led me to a small church and an altar call where I strained to speak in tongues. I tried desperately, I even tried to mutter something that might have been mistaken for a Phoenician dialect, but the message was all too dismal and clear: They also serve who only stand and wait, and in my case I was also supposed to be very, very quiet.

Retreating then into the interpersonal and mistaking it as the exclusive domain of the spiritual, I took comfort from being a part of this group family in which the first unwritten rule was dependence upon one another. Ultimately, though, we wearied of one another, like children cooped up on a day of rain. Tired of self-discovery, communal criticism, and the deferment of professional aspiration, we exhausted one another in all senses of the word—we became burnt-out cases, resigned to breed, pay our bills, and live the rest of our lives like our parents. By the time I left—and in order to pry myself away, I needed a pretext that was two thousand miles distant—I knew that I was forfeiting the most significant relationships of my life, the standard, nearly erotic in its intensity, by which I would measure subsequent connections and the loss of which I would always mourn. But I also knew—to put it in the vernacular—that I needed to get the hell out.

I did leave, but I suppose the shadow of that former life was bound to catch up with me sooner or later. I read the newspapers and watched the televised reports of the Heaven's Gate suicides, but I was unable to call them crackpots or fools. Deluded by a madman, they remained true to a collective conviction, blinded by a splendid vision only they could see or understand. Their bodies, grave reminders of dependence taken to an extreme, left the mansion in bags. When my wife and I left our community, it was with a psychic dislocation no less final. During our first weeks of freedom, we called weekly and wondered if we had made the greatest mistake of our lives. Is it so surprising that in the days and weeks following the suicides, there were others who, after separating from the group, chose to follow anyway? Watching the news, I felt a square of purple cloth cover my eyes.

That Saturday afternoon, my unacknowledged disturbance claimed its due: I grew deathly tired. After a brief nap that did not produce sleep so much as a viscous stupor, I knew that things were not at a good pass. I could call my parents to watch the children while I drove to the emergency room or I could set the living room on fire. We worked a jigsaw puzzle instead, my daughters and I—Alice in Wonderland sitting down to tea with the Mad Hatter and the March Hare—and before it was time to fix dinner I had the sense that the nameless ogre hammering upon my faculties had begun to lose interest; while still cracked and splintered, the pieces of my psyche were already beginning to reassemble themselves, a restoration that would take the balance of the weekend.

By the time my wife returned, my sense of equilibrium, at least in part, had returned as well. Except for the shadow of what I remembered feeling—or rather not feeling—I almost felt "normal." But what, I wonder, is "not-normal"? And where, or what, is the line that divides the two?

I am beginning to understand something of this new boundary: that I suffer from mild yet periodic visitations of depression, a melancholy brought on by the understanding that what I was convinced to be true is not altogether so. Through the passage of time, those periodic symptoms may grow into something truly troublesome. Believing that exercise may serve some prophylactic function better than Prozac, I swim laps and hope to keep the demons at bay. One night, the underwater light at the shallow end burned out, and the threadbare imagery of light and darkness was made new again. How odd to be swimming in the dark! Odder still were the transitions of light to dark and back again while in the same pool, the same water. The clarity of one end was magnified by the murk at the other, a flip-turn becoming an existential enterprise. In the shallow end I was prey to all kinds of neurotic foreboding—heart attack, aneurysm, drowning, my body left undiscovered until morning, my poor dear children!— while at the deep end in the light I could swim forever.

Is it not also possible that without a certain level of depression, it may be difficult to experience a measure of joy? Transcendent moments, after all, are difficult to measure or appreciate without their concomitant opposites: Wonderland must have its Underland. As metaphor cannot exist without a literal correlative, and the literal becomes dry without the imaginative infusion of metaphor, so too are heaven and earth offered to us as complementary entrees on the same plate. Without one we are perilously close to becoming like the followers of Heaven's Gate, so in thrall to the prospects of literal otherness, a literal abstraction, that we forsake the metaphor offered in the here-and-now.

Or, as in my own case, we become so apprehensive about listening to anything other than the sound of another human voice,

76

we fail to notice the few transcendent, personal moments available in any one lifetime. We run the risk of seeing God in the face of a child only to notice the dirty face and the uncombed hair. Or we respond to a burning bush by fetching the garden hose. Is it any wonder that the notion of grace can apply to God's mercy as well as to a perfectly executed tackle? The wonder is that we try so hard to separate the two.

CONSIDERATIONS

PAUL C. VITZ

EXPERIENCING THE SUPERNATURAL

A PROBLEM OF WILL

I WOULD LIKE TO ADDRESS THE SKEPTIC, the atheist, or the agnostic (and the doubter in all of us) who rejects both God and spiritual reality. Doubting the transcendent may seem to solve many intellectual dilemmas because it teaches us to rely on what we can know empirically—the data most easily transformed into technical solutions. Certainly the advent of the twentieth century brought with it tremendous hope that age-old problems of the human condition could best be addressed in this way.

I am convinced, however, that the rejection of God and the transcendent which figured so large at the start of modernity must be dealt with if we are to overcome our current dilemmas—from bioethical, to environmental, to social-political. The Western intellectual community has shown serious bias, it seems to me, in failing to bring these issues into the open. They ought to be part of the public debate. Many people are waking up to the possible linkage between spiritual questions and such problems as family collapse, crime, environmental degradation, and "predator youth." The collapse of ideologies such as Marxism, Freudianism, behaviorism, and the like is causing us to reassess many questions once thought disposed of, specifically the existence of God and humankind's ability to apprehend God. Therefore, the time, I believe, is ripe to make God and the spiritual life an active part of the contemporary intellectual agenda.

There need to be good reasons to do so, of course. Let's investigate a promising argument.

An important initial point is that throughout human history and its varied cultures three great external types of reality commonly have been assumed to exist. These are the external physical world, the world of other minds, and the transcendent spiritual world, for example, of God or the gods. An interesting feature that these three presumed realities share is that we cannot prove the existence of any of them.[1] Indeed, in 1967 the eminent philosopher Alvin Plantinga published *God and Other Minds*, in which he proved that the degree of rational uncertainty about the existence of other minds and about the existence of God is exactly the same. (This proof assumes what is called "classical foundationalism"—namely, that an argument or proof for God's existence is required, and that an acceptable argument is one derived from an original set of self-evident axioms.) Plantinga shows that the rational grounds for accepting the existence of God and other minds has the same structure and involves the same assumptions—assumptions that he then demonstrates are often question-begging. For example, we never directly experience other people's minds, and our assumption that they exist is based on an analogy with our own mental life.

Plantinga's proof itself is sophisticated and cannot be summarized easily, but its general structure is not hard to grasp. Plantinga first systematically shows that neither natural theology nor natural "atheology" offers a satisfying solution to the problem of a rational justification of belief in God's existence or of God's nonexistence. He then tries another approach to the justification of belief in God by exploring its analogies and connections with a similar problem, the "problem of other minds"; that is, how do you rationally justify the existence of other people's minds? Plantinga goes on to "defend the analogical argument for other minds against current criticism and argues that it is as good an answer as we have to the question of other minds. But . . . it turns out that the analogical argument finally succumbs to a malady exactly resembling the one afflicting the teleological argument [for God's existence]."[2]

The malady is that the analogical argument—derived from our own mental life—proves too much. That is, the argument can prove not only that other minds exist and feel pain, but also that the mind can feel all pains, and so on. Since we do not feel all pains, or remember all past experiences, the argument must be wrong. Likewise the same argument for God's existence proves too much. Plantinga concludes that "belief in other minds and belief in God are in the same epistemological boat; hence if either is rational, so is the other. But obviously the former is rational; so, therefore, is the latter."[3] His formal proof for this conclusion has stood without a successful challenge for some thirty years.

In his more recent work, Plantinga shows that, just as we cannot prove the existence of other minds, it is also impossible to prove the existence of external physical reality or even to prove the existence of the past. Again, he shows that the failure in each proof is identical to the failure of the teleological argument for God's existence. One obvious implication of Plantinga's work is that if scientists tend to accept the existence of physical reality and of other minds, but to reject that of God, then this is done on nonrational grounds. Before we turn to some of the nonrational reasons behind the rejection of the spiritual realm, it will be useful to discuss how it is that the existence of the external world is commonly accepted. First, the problem of proving the existence of external reality arises once one accepts the fact that our knowledge of external reality is always mediated by the nervous system: All we are directly aware of is our own states of mind. We must—we can only—infer an external reality existing behind and acting as a cause of our sensations, perception, and so on. But the validity of this inference is what cannot be proved. We may accept Plantinga's reasoning in this matter or we may be convinced on other grounds that proving the existence of the physical world is not possible. There are, of course, many skeptics on this issue in Western philosophy; for example, the writings of David Hume, Bishop Berkeley, and Thomas Reid certainly support Plantinga's conclusion on this issue.

Nevertheless, almost no one has ever doubted physical reality to the point of trying seriously to live by such a position. Someone who lived on the basis of such doubt should not bother to eat food and would surely walk into walls, fall into ditches, and make other such blunders. A few idealist philosophers seem to be the intellectual representatives of a position that does deny or comes close to denying the physical world, but they do it only in their lectures and writings, not in their daily lives.

The overwhelming majority of scientists, not to mention ordinary citizens of the world, have always accepted the existence of an external physical reality. Scientific theories are, after all, about something outside of us. The grounds for this acceptance seem to be that we are so made that sensory and perceptual *experience* carries with it the completely convincing notion that we are experiencing external reality. Put somewhat differently: Our normal interaction with what appears to be physical reality naturally creates a firm conviction of its existence. Of course, in some rare instances one's perception of external reality may be faulty. There are such things as illusions and hallucinations. But even these errors are observed, noted, and corrected by more refined and systematic perceptual contact with the same presumed external world. Hence, to believe that the whole realm of physical reality does not exist, or that most, or even much, of our perceptual experience is without an external source, is rightly considered bizarre. Except for certain kinds of philosophers, such as the above-mentioned idealists, who are given a kind of philosopher's license, at least briefly, to suspend common sense, anyone who fails to believe in the external world is judged as suffering from a mental pathology.

Likewise, our belief in the existence of other minds comes from interaction with other people. Sensory contact with a person, plus interaction involving language and symbolic communication, appears adequate to persuade us of the existence of other minds.

It is important to note that a crucial issue with respect to initiating and maintaining contact with external physical reality or with other minds is whether the person has the *will* or *desire* to initiate the interaction with the presumed reality. For example, suppose you find a man who is on an artificial respirator in a darkened room and who believes there is no external reality. After some investigation you discover that he has not walked or used his eyes or ears for some time. You desire to cure him of this intellectual ailment—one obviously supported by his markedly reduced physical and perceptual activity. A reasonable strategy would be to get him to open his eyes and unstop his ears, and to. talk with him often. In time you, his guide, would encourage him to strengthen his muscles and begin to walk so that he could come out of his room and enter the outside world. Therapy for his pathological intellectual position is thus to immerse him in direct interaction with the reality that he denies. In this case, there is every reason to believe that such a program would convince him of the reality of the physical world. But such a procedure depends upon his willingness to cooperate with you in interacting with the outside world. As for logical proof, that would remain, as always, impossible.

Now let us suppose we find someone who denies that other minds exist and lives as though other minds do not exist. (Such a position, of course, seems to be quite rare, so rare that I have never heard of its existence.) However, let us also suppose we have found such a person and that our subject's condition is strongly supported by his social isolation. He lives alone and has for years; he never speaks to anyone, and he appears to have withdrawn completely from interpersonal communication. As a result, his lack of belief in other minds is not that surprising. He remembers interacting with people when he was young, but these experiences he attributes to a childish and immature understanding of things at the time. Again, this man's condition is fundamentally pathological, and correction would involve the introduction of interpersonal communication into his life. In time he would discover friends and enemies; perhaps he would even love or hate. Later, after years of friendship, if he were to be reminded by an old friend of his former belief that other minds do not exist, his only answer might be to look at his friend and laugh. In short, interaction with other minds is necessary in order to accept their existence; apparently in all known cases this interaction is sufficient.

Let me suggest that the situation with respect to belief in the transcendent spiritual realm is similar. First, note that most of the people who consistently deny the existence not only of God but indeed of the entire spiritual realm constitute a relatively small group that seems to have come into existence in Western Europe about 250 years ago. Most of them have been trained in science or other rationalistic and intellectual disciplines. They tend to work in universities or certain professions that are highly specialized and often involve peculiar environments. They tend to socialize mostly with those having similar skeptical outlooks. What they mean by "real thinking" is the mental manipulation of abstract written symbols, often numbers, or other very digital elements. To such people a proper belief system or world view is something constructed by the correct sequencing of these symbols with occasional checks on whether some kind of observation backs it up. That is, their world view is something that exists in a digital code, and they seem to assume that digital codes are adequate for representing any kind of question, problem, or knowledge. The very notion of a belief system based on perceptual information coded in the body and often unavailable to conscious verbal expression, or on a world view based significantly on direct personal experience, does not occur to them.

Also striking is the fact that these people never or almost never go to church or synagogue or read religious writings. But most peculiar of all is that they appear never to pray, to meditate, or to engage in other spiritual exercises. That is, they rarely, if ever, use the well-known procedures for getting and staying in contact with the transcendent spiritual realm.

Again, the answer to this pathology is not some logical attempt to prove the existence of God or of spiritual reality. As in the cases of the physical world and other minds, this is impossible anyway. The answer is to try and convince such a person to pray: that is, to talk with God, to listen for God's voice, or to engage in other spiritual activities. If such a person refuses to interact with the transcendent and is determined to remain in spiritual isolation, there is little one can do. This requirement that one engage in prayer and meditation is a serious one. For example, if someone doubted some astronomical or physical claim—such as the existence of moons around Jupiter or the reality of a whole level of physical existence (e.g., of subatomic particles)—an honest search for an answer would require a number of steps. First, the person, if ignorant of astronomy or physics, would need a guide—a trained scientist—and would have to become at least something of an amateur scientist. It would take considerable time and commitment from the seeker. After all, observations are often ambiguous; in any case, observations do not reliably interpret themselves. Even more important, a person who denied the very existence of the external world would be unqualified to judge the validity of physical knowledge; likewise, a person who did not believe in the existence of other minds could not be an adequate psychologist.[4]

In almost all religious and spiritual traditions a knowledgeable person—a guide, if you will—is needed. And prayer and meditation are the primary instruments, the "telescopes," for contacting or interacting with spiritual reality. No scientist who refuses to seek religious experience has the intellectual right to say that spiritual reality does not exist or that the mind cannot be affected by that reality. A person who has had no religious experience is simply unqualified to comment on the existence, much less the nature, of spiritual phenomena. Please note, I am not saying that the person must have a particular interpretation or understanding of his religious or spiritual experience—only that he must have had a reasonable amount of such experience. Perhaps after various religious experiences the person will conclude it was all an illusion or something other than what it first appeared to be. Fine. Scientific observations, too, can be mistaken; there are such things as artifacts. Particular spiritual experiences can also be artifacts, or perhaps even all such experience is illusory. However, a scientist who has no systematic empirical understanding of a phenomenon is not in a position to give informed criticism. And a scientist who was ignorant of and refused to become involved with the experimental methodology used to demonstrate that a major phenomenon existed would be considered incompetent to evaluate the claim. If he actively persisted in rejecting the phenomenon on a priori grounds, his colleagues would rightfully dismiss his claims as unqualified, even should subsequent research prove his position to be right.

I trust the argument is clear. Religion for most people is supported by religious or spiritual experience in which people claim a relationship or interaction with a spiritual realm, in particular with "spiritual minds." This may mean interaction with God, or Jesus, or with a dead person, or even with evil spirits. To evaluate the validity of these extremely important claims requires that an investigator seek contact with spiritual reality. There are various ways people do this, but first they must have the *will* to seek. The desire to seek, of course, is something rooted in psychological factors and has relatively little to do with what we usually refer to by such terms as "reason" or "evidence."[5]

This issue of having the will to seek interaction with spiritual reality is a very important one. For example, the prominent American intellectual and philosopher Mortimer Adler frequently wrote about the case for belief in God, but pulled back from accepting such belief. In his autobiography Adler wrote that his reluctance "[lay] in the state of one's will, not in the state of one's mind." And he admitted that to become seriously religious "would require a radical change in my way of life.... The simple truth of the matter is I did not wish to live up to being a genuinely religious person."[6]

Countless other atheists and skeptics presumably suffer from the same motivational weakness. They are likely, however, to disguise their problem as due to the evidence of modern science or some other similar "reason." And, of course, many atheists and skeptics are extraordinarily superficial in their motives for unbelief. This understanding is well described by the Baron d'Holbach, the French Enlightenment philosopher and perhaps the first public atheist. But though an atheist, he was very critical of many nonbelievers. He wrote: "We must allow that corruption of manners, debauchery, license, and even frivolity of mind may often lead to irreligion or infidelity. . . . These pretended free-thinkers have examined nothing for themselves; they rely on others whom they suppose to have weighed matters more carefully. How can men, given up to voluptuousness and debauchery, plunged in excess, ambitions, intriguing, frivolous, and dissipated—or depraved women of wit and fashion—how can such as these be capable of forming an opinion of a religion they have never thoroughly examined?"[7]

Presumably such motivation is very prevalent today, especially in the media and entertainment industries. One is reminded of Psalm 14: "The fool says in his heart, 'There is no God.'"

Sigmund Freud wrote as follows in his critique of religion, *The Future of an Illusion*: "If the truth of religious doctrines is dependent on inner experience which bears witness to that truth, what is one to do about the many people who do not have this rare experience?"[8] The problem with Freud's lament is that, first, religious experience is far from rare and, second, Freud himself never sought God or religious experience. Freud was unwilling to seek; thus, he did not find, nor should he or we be surprised at his predictable failure. At best, Freud's complaint is foolish, at worst, dishonest.

In any case, given the will to seek, the most common instruments or techniques for contact with spiritual reality are prayer and meditation; they are the "telescopes" of the religious person. No truth-seeker should be afraid to look through any kind of telescope. Another way to put it is to note that in the United States some 95 percent of the population say they believe in God. Every year millions of people in the United States alone have personally significant religious experiences. To ignore evaluating this obviously relevant information is an act of intellectual denial that boggles the mind.

The major reason for raising the question of spiritual experience is its relevance to the social and moral dilemmas of our postmodern age. These dilemmas have taken many years to unfold, and no doubt they will take many years to resolve. I am convinced, however, that until we humans can regain the perspective of our intermediate place in reality, there is no way to deal with our crisis. That intermediate position is between God and nature while being thoroughly connected to both. Thus, many of our problems today come from a self-preoccupation derived from an intellectual misunderstanding of who we are. We are not autonomous and alone; instead we are part of nature interacting with the external world, and we are part of our relationships with other minds. Our purpose is transcendent, derived from interaction with God. To once again accept this ancient wisdom, the modern intellectual community will have to address the reality of the transcendent—in particular, God.

NOTES

1   Certain Catholic philosophers do believe it is possible to prove the existence of God. If this is true, then the present argument is irrelevant and the problem is the bias of modern intellectuals. However, the failure of so many thinkers to accept such a proof is probably evidence that the proof is unsatisfactory.

2   A. Plantinga, *God and Other Minds* (Ithaca: Cornell University Press, 1967), viii.

3   Ibid.

4   Certain forms of extreme behaviorism at least in theory came close to denying the existence of other minds. However, such positions were rare, and appear to be nonexistent today; in any case this kind of behaviorism made for a grossly inadequate psychology.

5   For a book treating the psychological factors behind atheism, see the forthcoming *The Psychological Origins of Atheism* by Paul C. Vitz (Dallas: Spence).

6   M. Adler, *Philosopher at Large: An Intellectual Biography* (New York: Macmillan, 1977), 316.

7   *Système de la Nature*, tom. ii, chap. 13; quoted in N. Laforet, *The Causes and Cure of Unbelief*, rev. and ed. by J. Gibbons (Boston: Thomas J. Flynn, 1909), 123.

8   S. Freud, *The Future of an Illusion*, trans. and ed. by J. Strackey (New York: Norton, 1961), 28.

PHILLIP E. JOHNSON

DARWIN AND THE SUPERNATURAL

CONTACT WITH THE SPIRITS

CARL SAGAN WAS PROBABLY THE WORLD'S most influential proponent of scientific materialism at the time of his death in 1997, although Richard Dawkins and Stephen Jay Gould would also be candidates for that dubious honor. "The Cosmos is all there is, or ever was, or ever will be," Sagan famously pronounced in his popular *Cosmos* series, which has been presented as the Word of Science to hundreds of millions of schoolchildren around the world. Sagan was also the world's most famous debunker of such things as fortune-tellers and UFO sightings. One of his favorite targets was Dr. John Mack, the Harvard Medical School psychiatrist who believes that some of his patients really have been kidnapped by space aliens. Nonetheless, the final product of Sagan's life—the movie version of his novel *Contact*—combines a variant of the alien abduction story with the occult theme of communication with the spirits of the dead. It is as if Sagan were determined to contradict himself and to find room for what amounts to witchcraft within the territory of the scientific imagination.

Consider the basic plot line of *Contact*. The scientist hero Ellie Arroway appears at the beginning as a girl devoted to her widower father and to her ham radio set. When the father dies of a sudden heart attack, Ellie spurns the inept comforting words of an unctuous clergyman; her father died because she failed to get the heart medicine to him in time. (In keeping with standard Hollywood practice, Christians in this movie are all repulsive characters.) Henceforth Ellie will look to science to find meaning in life—and also to find out what happens after death. She goes directly from the funeral to her ham radio set to try to contact her dead father. Her subsequent career as a scientist, fanatically devoted to Carl Sagan's real-life Search for Extraterrestrial Intelligence (SETI) project, is thus a logical outgrowth of her juvenile effort at communication with the spirit world. Ellie goes into science for the kind of reason that might lead another to visit a spirit medium or to join a charismatic religious movement.

Religion and romance appear in the film together in the persona of Palmer Joss, a combination hunk, New Age guru, and political manipulator. Palmer's God has nothing to do with morality as conventionally understood, a point he makes dramatically by taking Ellie to bed on their first date. Although his theology is as cloudy as his morality (the pages of his "Bible" are blank), Palmer stands for reliance upon faith and personal trust in opposition to Ellie's cold scientific rationalism. When Ellie's SETI project finally hits pay dirt, by receiving an alien communication containing blueprints for a bizarre spaceship, Palmer (now a Presidential adviser) torpedoes her dream of being the astronaut to make contact with the aliens by somehow convincing an international panel that she is an unsuitable representative of earth's population because she does not believe in God. After a still more preposterous subplot involving a Christian terrorist (of course!) and a creepy billionaire who is a cross between Howard Hughes and Armand Hammer, Ellie ends up with the astronaut job anyway.

The immensely expensive alien-designed machine takes Ellie to a distant part of the universe, where she finds herself on a beach and has a joyous reunion with her dead father—except that it is not really her father but an emissary from an alien civilization, packaged this way with the aid of data taken from her own memories. (In principle this technology could deliver something like immortality, by downloading human minds into imperishable computers.) The father/alien delivers a banal message ("all we have is each other") that could just as easily have been sent to earth by radio at much less cost. The mystery of the purpose of all this treasury-busting space travel deepens when Ellie returns to earth. To earthbound observers, nothing happened and the space vehicle went nowhere. Like a beatific vision, the voyage to the beyond took place only in Ellie's subjectivity, and she can present no evidence that it was anything but a hallucination.

The consummate scientific rationalist thus finds herself having to tell skeptical investigators that they should believe her personal testimony despite the contrary objective data. Palmer now redeems himself by saying he believes her, and the fickle public puts its credulousness to good use for once by rallying around Ellie and spurning the rationalists. (The triumphal scene calls to mind the crowds in Jerusalem on Palm Sunday.) In the end the conflict between faith and science evaporates, because we learn that the spaceship's electronic records, suppressed for no apparent reason by the government (of course!), show a mysterious time gap and thus substantiate Ellie's story after all. It is as if Dr. John Mack had been spectacularly vindicated by the discovery of an unimpeachably genuine videotape of an alien abduction, long buried in a top-secret NASA vault by order of Carl Sagan.

Finally, the book version of *Contact* (but not the movie) ends with Ellie's computer finding a geometric message, hidden in the infinite decimal numbers of *pi* many "kilometers downstream of the decimal point." The message proves conclusively that "there is an intelligence that antedates the universe." It seems that, after all, the Cosmos is not all there is, or was, or ever will be. In the beginning was the Word.

The contradictory messages of Carl Sagan's fiction and his popular science writing appropriately reflect the confused relationship of empirical science with the supernatural. If we define "God" as the intelligence that antedates the physical universe, does science validate the existence of such an intelligence, or negate it, or confine its activities to the ultimate beginning of time—or does science have nothing at all to say to us about this most important of subjects? We can find arguments for all of these positions in the writings of leading scientists. A related question of importance is how we are to tell the difference between real (i.e., reliable) science and the kind of pseudo-science that counterfeits the good name of science while avoiding the crucial requirement of testing by repeatable experiments. Does bad science come more often from affirming the reality of the supernatural, or from overextending the reach of materialist explanations in order to exclude the supernatural?

In a brilliant retrospective essay on Carl Sagan's career, Harvard genetics professor Richard Lewontin, wrote approvingly that the essence of Sagan's message was that "We exist as material beings in a material world, all of whose phenomena are the consequences of physical relations among material entities."[1] With unconscious irony, Lewontin wrote that "As one bit of evidence for the bad state of public consciousness, Sagan cites opinion polls showing that the majority of Americans believe that extraterrestrials have landed from UFO's."[2] We can only suppose that this majority will have increased substantially now that the credulous multitudes have digested the message of *Contact*. There is no doubt that science has done much to discredit superstition, but sometimes the scientific imagination merely substitutes new materialist superstitions for the old supernatural ones. In place of witchcraft and devil worship, we get psychoanalysis, Marxism, social Darwinism, and space aliens. These materialist delusions pop up to fill the spiritual void left by a philosophy that can expel one kind of superstition, but cannot satisfy our spiritual needs. The situation of the modern materialist was best described in Jesus' parable of the unclean spirit:

> Now when the unclean spirit goes out of a man, it passes through waterless places, seeking rest, and does not find it. Then it says, "I will return to my house from which I came"; and when it comes, it finds it unoccupied, swept, and put in order. Then it goes, and takes along with it seven other spirits more wicked than itself, and they go in and live there; and the last state of that man becomes worse than the first. (Matt. 12:43-46, NASB)

The Twilight of Darwinism

To understand why science sometimes discredits and sometimes creates myth and superstition, we need to realize that our culture employs two conflicting definitions of "science." On the one hand, science is said to be a process of rigorous testing, in which hypotheses are confirmed or discredited by repeatable experiments. On the other hand, science is identified in the minds of many with materialistic philosophy. That philosophy by definition attempts to explain the entire history of the universe in materialistic terms, if necessary by theories that are not testable or even remotely plausible. When science is defined as applied materialist philosophy, it automatically excludes the possibility of divine action, regardless of the evidence. Materialist science can be remarkably tolerant of unverified materialist theories, provided that they play a useful role in supporting the claim that a science based on materialism is the only valid way of comprehending reality. For example, here is how Richard Lewontin describes the fundamental problem of science education:

> People believe a lot of nonsense about the world of phenomena, nonsense that is a consequence of a wrong way of thinking. . . . [T]he problem is to get them to reject irrational and supernatural explanations of the world, the demons that exist only in their imaginations, and to accept a social and intellectual apparatus, Science, as the only begetter of truth.[3]

Lewontin recognizes that, for science to be the only begetter of truth, the world has to be composed only of material entities, which may be defined as the kind of particles that physicists identify and study. The creed of scientific materialism thus starts with the dogmatic affirmation that "In the beginning were the particles, and the impersonal natural laws of physics and chemistry." In the materialist universe there could not have been a mind at the beginning, because mind could only exist after it had first evolved from mindless matter. Matter therefore had to be able to do its own creating, including the creating of the immense quantity of genetic information that exists in biological organisms.

Let's stop to consider just how difficult a job of creation that was. According to Richard Dawkins, the most prominent living spokesman for Darwinism and scientific materialism, "Biology is the study of complicated things that give the appearance of having been designed for a purpose." Francis Crick, one of the world's most eminent living biologists and an equally fervent materialist, admits in his autobiography that "Biologists have to constantly remind themselves that the things they study were not designed, but evolved." The implication seems to be that the appearance of design would overwhelm the biologists if they ever forgot to keep reminding themselves. Crick himself simply gave up on evolution when he tried to explain how various kinds of bacteria could have evolved on the early earth. Even the simplest living creatures exhibit so many types of complexity, he reasoned, that they could not have evolved on earth in the time available but must have been sent here in a spaceship by a dying alien civilization. That's essentially a materialist version of supernatural creation.

Richard Dawkins is also frank about the difficulty of explaining the information content of living organisms by an unintelligent material process:

> Physics books may be complicated, but . . . the objects and phenomena that a physics book describes are simpler than a single cell in the body of its author. And the author consists of trillions of those cells, many of them different from each other, organized with intricate architecture and precision-engineering into a working machine capable of writing a book. . . .

> Each nucleus . . . contains a digitally coded database larger, in information content, than all 30 volumes of the *Encyclopedia Britannica* put together. And this figure is for each cell, not all the cells of the body put together.[4]

Putting the problem in terms of "information content" invites us to draw an analogy to a book or to a computer program. I typed this article on a word processor, using a complex word processing program and an even more complex operating system (Windows 95), on computer hardware that was designed by an advanced engineering technology. Neither the information in my article, nor the information in any of the supporting computer software and hardware, ever could have been produced by unintelligent material processes. You do not get a manuscript without an author, and you do not get a word processor or a desktop computer without teams of highly educated engineers. What is more, the immense informational content involved in producing a meaningful text has to be matched by equally impressive equipment for interpreting the information. If you did not have visual and neural equipment that is far more complex than any computer, the writing on this page would be as meaningless to you as the pattern of dust flecks on an unswept floor. This need for the transmitter and the receiver to appear together is important to keep in mind when discussing (for example) the evolution of the eye, which requires the simultaneous appearance of not only the sensory apparatus but also the neural mechanisms necessary to interpret the sense data and act upon it.

Darwinists insist that, although the manuscript and the word processor both require a designer, the far more complex biological systems in my body and yours were produced by unintelligent material processes, specifically the Darwin mechanism of mutation and selection. For the Darwinian claim to be even conceivably true, two stringent requirements would have to be met. First, random mutation would have to be a generator of complex information, meaning information as complex as all the neural machinery in the brain cells of that physicist. Do not be distracted from this essential point by any references to natural selection. Natural selection is nothing more than nonrandom death, and death does not provide genetic information or anything else that is new. All the positive input in evolution has to be contributed by new mutations, or by recombination of the information previously contributed by old mutations. Natural selection comes into the picture only in meeting the second requirement: There must be a continuous path of viable intermediate forms all the way from the putative starting point (say, a bacterium) to its putative descendants (say, a tree, a worm, a lobster, and a human). Evolution from simple to complex must proceed by gradual steps, each an adaptive improvement upon its predecessors, if it is to proceed at all.

Dawkins's example of the thirty-volume encyclopedia provides a good illustration of the Darwinian theory of how genetic information might be produced. It is statistically impossible to produce the information in the thirty volumes by a single random combination of the letters of the English alphabet, even though a lot of information is already present if we are allowed to start with those highly artificial letters already in existence. A random assortment of letters might produce a single word, however—or even, after a vast number of tries, a coherent English phrase or short sentence. If somehow each useful word or phrase that appears in a useful order could be preserved, then in an immense amount of time we might build up, phrase by phrase, a page, a chapter, and even a coherent book.

The crucial criterion to meet the requirements of materialist philosophy is that the process of information-building must be entirely unintelligent. For that reason, it will not do to imagine (as Dawkins does) a scenario in which a computer program selects the words for preservation by comparing them to a target book in its memory. Selection by computer program is selection by intelligence, and it depends for success on a programmer who determines the outcome. The same is true of domestic animal breeding, which requires the participation of a skilled human intelligence to recognize the genetic variants and protect them from unforgiving nature, which would otherwise quickly eliminate them. "Natural selection" is thus a profoundly misleading term, since anything that had the ability to "select" would be intelligent and hence disqualified from participation in evolution.

The reality behind the mystique of natural selection is merely that some organisms—not necessarily those with the most complex genetic information—are better at surviving and reproducing than others, and the genes of the survivors will dominate succeeding generations. This unremarkable truth has no necessary connection with increasing complexity or the origin of intelligence, as is evident from the fact that lowly bacteria, apparently fundamentally unchanged since the earliest times, are vastly more capable than chimps or even humans at the essential Darwinian business of reproducing their kind. The existence of all the necessary adaptive steps required for the Darwinian mechanism to create complex plants and animals is merely a hypothesis in the theory, unconfirmed and unconfirmable.

Darwinism has a powerful appeal to the imagination of persons, whether they are biologists or not, who want a strictly materialist theory of biological creation that keeps God at a safe distance from the business of life. This factor explains why it survives despite what otherwise would be devastating scientific refutations. Mutation has never been shown to be a source of new genetic information at all, let alone in the fantastic quantity required for the Darwinian scenario. Mutations in DNA sequences, like random changes in a computer program, tend to decrease the amount of usable information. Even induced mutations, as in the extensive experiments with fruitflies, are effective only at producing defects, and mutations have never even begun to reprogram the process of development to create a new viable creature of a different kind. Embryonic development, in which many Darwinists still imagine they find traces of evolutionary history (such as the imaginary "gills" in human embryos), turns out to be utterly inconsistent with Darwinian expectations. Supposedly closely related organisms have early developmental patterns that are radically different, and specific characteristics that are supposedly "homologous" (derived from common ancestors) often develop in the descendants from different sites in the embryos.

The fossil record always has been overwhelmingly anti-Darwinian, despite the determined efforts of paleontologists to construe every doubtful piece of evidence as support for the theory. The controversy of the "punctuated equilibria" theory in the 1980s brought this long-concealed fact to public attention. Fossil studies today still show overwhelmingly, as they did in Darwin's time, that the most unmistakable characteristic of the fossil record is stasis, meaning the absence of fundamental evolutionary change. When new groups appear in the rocks they appear suddenly, without a record of gradual development from something else, and thereafter they remain essentially unchanged. Although the official explanation for this embarrassing fact is that the fossil record is incomplete, the record most conclusively refutes the Darwinian story of gradual directional changes just where it is most complete, in the case of marine vertebrates that lived in the shallow seas and hence were frequently fossilized.

Science or Materialism?

The interesting question is not whether Darwinism fits the scientific evidence; it clearly does not. The interesting question is how a theory so plainly at variance with the evidence can survive, and even dominate the universities and the mass media. Richard Lewontin provides the answer:

> We take the side of science [i.e., evolutionary science] in spite of the patent absurdity of some of its constructs, ... in spite of the tolerance of the scientific community for unsubstantiated just-so stories, because we have a prior commitment, a commitment to materialism. It is not that the methods and institutions of science somehow compel us to accept a material explanation of the phenomenal world, but, on the contrary, that we are forced by our a priori adherence to material causes to create an apparatus of investigation and a set of concepts that produce material explanations, no matter how counterintuitive, no matter how mystifying to the uninitiated. Moreover, that materialism is absolute, for we cannot allow a Divine Foot in the door. The eminent Kant scholar Lewis Beck used to say that anyone who could believe in God could believe in anything. To appeal to an omnipotent deity is to allow that at any moment the regularities of nature may be ruptured, that miracles may happen.[5]

The mistake made by most people who accept Darwinism, including theistic evolutionists, is to suppose that for evolutionary scientists the facts come first and the materialist philosophy comes afterwards. As Lewontin explains, this has it exactly backwards. The alleged creative power of natural selection was never inferred from evidence, but rather deduced from the requirements of materialist philosophy. As I have put it elsewhere: If Darwinism is the answer, what is the question? The question is: How could all the necessary creating have been done without God? Contemporary science starts with the correct premise that God is outside of the realm accessible to science, and from that premise leaps to the non sequitur that all evidence of God's existence is also outside of science.

On the contrary, the evidence of biology speaks everywhere for intelligent design—when the evidence is viewed without materialist bias. The best known recent example is Lehigh University molecular biologist Michael Behe's 1996 book *Darwin's Black Box.*[6] Behe shows that the invisible world of molecular systems is replete with examples of irreducible complexity, meaning systems composed of many complex parts, all of which have to be present at once for any part to perform a useful function. Such systems cannot be built up part by part through the mindless Darwinian process, which (assuming it is capable of producing a part in the first place) cannot preserve a presently unuseful part in the hope that it will become useful at some time in the future.

Behe's writing is controversial in the scientific community, not because of anything he says about the scientific evidence, but because he dares to draw the inference that the presence of irreducible complexity implies the reality of the designer. But Behe is not the only molecular biologist who knows that the facts of biology are fatal to Darwinism. James Shapiro of the

University of Chicago, who refuses to draw any theistic implications from his findings, nonetheless paints a scientific picture highly similar to Behe's in a 1997 article in the *Boston Review* with the provocative title "Scientific Alternatives to Darwinism: Is There a Role for Cellular Information Processing in Evolution?" [7]

Just to give the flavor of Shapiro's article, here is a string of excerpts:

> [T]he molecular revolution has revealed an unanticipated realm of complexity and interaction more consistent with computer technology than with the mechanical viewpoint which dominated when the neo-Darwinian Modern Synthesis was formulated. . . . It has been a surprise to learn how thoroughly cells protect themselves against the kinds of accidental genetic change that, according to conventional theory, are the sources of evolutionary variability. . . . The point of this discussion is that our current knowledge of genetic change is fundamentally at variance with postulates held by neo-Darwinists. . . . Is there any guiding intelligence at work in the origin of species displaying exquisite adaptations that range from lambda prophage repression and the Krebs cycle through the mitotic apparatus and the eye to the immune system, mimicry, and social organization?

In short, the facts point away from the guiding materialist philosophy and toward the reality of design. Scientific materialists such as Richard Lewontin find it difficult to recognize this situation because they identify the supernatural with the irrational. If God exists then miracles can happen; materialists think that this possibility means the end of science because it implies that all events are subject to arbitrary forces that science cannot comprehend. But of course this is nonsense. What threatens the integrity of the mind, including the scientific mind, is materialism itself. If matter is all there is, and the world and all its phenomena are the products of physical and chemical interactions, then the mind and its concepts are also the products of mindless material forces. In that case, what basis can we have for trusting our minds or for believing that our theories are true? Scientific materialists today are astonished at the extent to which irrationalist philosophies such as deconstruction have taken over the universities. They should not be, because those philosophies are merely reflections of the implications of materialism itself.

Science is fundamentally the story of the comprehending mind, and the only metaphysical platform that can support the reliability of the mind is the doctrine that humans are created in the image of God. We have the capacity to know Truth, because truth, with that capital *T*, is truth as God sees it. Because of our defects we see through a glass darkly, but it is only because of that divine image in us that we can see at all.

Supernatural action is not irrational action, unless you are an animist or pagan who believes in an anarchist divine realm of warring spirits. For the Christian or Jewish monotheist, God is the author of rationality and also the lawmaker who enacts the regularities that science studies. Intelligent causes in biology, just like intelligent causes in authorship or in computer design, are not arbitrary causes. A computer is manifestly the product of intelligent design, and yet it is no less regular in operation and accessible to scientific investigation. The same is true of biological organisms, including the minds and bodies of Carl Sagan, Richard Dawkins, and Richard Lewontin. Scripture teaches us that God's eternal power and divine majesty are visible in the things that have been made, and the evidence of science, as distinguished from the philosophy that currently dominates science, everywhere confirms that this teaching is true.

NOTES

1 Richard Lewontin, "Billions and Billions of Demons", review of *The Demon-Haunted World: Science as a Candle in the Dark*, by Carl Sagan, *The New York Review of Books*, 44.1 (Jan. 9, 1997): 28.

2 Ibid.

3 Ibid.

4 Richard Dawkins, *The Blind Watchmaker* (London: Longman, 1986), 2–3.

5 Lowentin, 31.

6 Michael J. Behe, *Darwin's Black Box: The Biochemical Challenge to Evolution* (New York: The Free Press, 1996).

7 The *Boston Review* is available on the web at <http://www.polisci.mit.edu/BostonReview/>.

DEAL W. HUDSON

THE PHILOSOPHER AND THE SUPERNATURAL

ANYONE FAMILIAR WITH EVEN THE VAGUEST OUTLINE of the history of ideas will recall that philosophers were not always so prejudiced against the supernatural. A philosophy that "began in wonder," as it did among the Greeks, was not so insistent on distancing itself from divine things. Socrates, who dropped by the temple each day in respect to the gods, used his final breath not for romantic self-congratulation, but for an act of piety: "Crito, we ought to offer a cock to Asclepius. See to it, and don't forget."

It is easy to ignore Socrates' last gesture as dramatic window-dressing, or, if pressed, to dismiss it as the residual taint of a primitive superstitious habit that philosophy would overthrow in the course of time. Many would undoubtedly argue that the history of philosophy is little less than a purgation, the gradual elimination of supposedly alien, supernatural elements from the rigor of philosophical reflection. Indeed, what is often identified with so-called "Enlightenment reason" is the conviction that philosophy by its very nature, as a mode of reflection on reality, eliminates any residue of religious belief or mysticism from philosophy itself or, for that matter, from the philosopher.

As we shall see, this characterization of philosophy is grossly inadequate, since it cuts philosophy off from its own history, from the philosopher himself, and from the very goal of wisdom—*sophia*—that is built into its name. In the attempt to demarcate the boundaries of its nature, philosophers have ignored "state," the actual concrete manner in which philosophy is exercised in the philosopher in his given time. Philosophy is not exercised by timeless angels in a heavenly realm of essences beyond time and space. Philosophy is practiced by specific philosophers who live a temporal, embodied existence of a specific time and place. The gradual exclusion of the supernatural from philosophy for the sake of defending its supposed nature has removed the philosopher from the sources of his deepest wisdom.

The Consensus Against Faith

Before the emergence of postmodernism, with its leading gurus Jacques Derrida and Michel Foucault, Bertrand Russell was the modern philosopher who most aggressively eliminated the supernatural from the philosophical enterprise. Russell successfully preached his philosophy-is-only-for-atheists message to several generations of post-war twentieth-century readers. His often brilliant but eccentric *The History of Western Philosophy* scornfully dismisses any philosophical figures who thematize their supernatural concerns. Russell's ignorance of the theological matters he so breezily commented upon was skillfully exposed by the great Jesuit historian of philosophy, Frederick Copleston. Russell's debate with Copleston on the existence of God is not widely known, although it was published and is available on audiotape.[1] But unlike C. S. Lewis, who admitted his philosophical limitations after his public thrashing by philosopher Elizabeth Anscombe, Russell never questioned the confidence of his basic convictions. And it showed in his writings: In fact, his celebrated *Why I Am Not a Christian* is so poorly argued that its effect on a number of readers, including myself, has been quite the opposite of Russell's intention.

Russell was not alone in his popularizing a philosophy devoid of intercourse with the supernatural. Will Durant, an important popularizer of the same generation, published his widely read *The Story of Philosophy: Lives and Opinions of the Great Philosophers*, with its awkward adulation of the atheistic Anton Schopenhauer. During the same period, however, there were other figures who continued working in the areas of the philosophy of religion, philosophical theology, and related disciplines. Probably the most influential of these, at least in academic philosophy, were the religious existentialists—Martin Heidegger, Karl Jaspers, Paul Tillich, and Gabriel Marcel—and the Catholic neo-Thomists—Etienne Gilson, Yves R. Simon, and Jacques Maritain—who dominated Catholic intellectual life from after World War I until Vatican II in the early 1960s.

Among the more widely read figures of his generation, it was Mortimer J. Adler who was the antidote to Russell. Adler, born into a nominally Jewish family, sought to give faith and religious experience an important place in both his dialectical research and his own account of reality. As an undergraduate at Columbia University, Adler decided to become a philosopher after reading the treatise on God in Saint Thomas Aquinas's *Summa*

Theologica. His intellectual conversion to the world of Aristotle and Aquinas, recounted in *Philosopher at Large: An Intellectual Biography*, led him to a brilliant early career among the small world of Catholic philosophers, including close friendships with the major Catholic intellectuals of his day, notably Jacques Maritain.

Later, Adler brought the common sense of Aristotle, but not the faith of Aquinas, to the Great Books movement he helped to found. For many years, Adler was asked why he never became a Christian. Adler would always explain that he lacked the gift of faith necessary to sincere religious belief. He had the "will to believe," as William James said, but not the supernatural gift necessary to trust in God's word. His sudden realization that he had received that gift at age eighty-five while lying in the bed of a Chicago hospital is memorably recorded in the second volume of his memoirs, *A Second Look in the Rearview Mirror.* Adler's life story serves as a powerful reminder of the importance of keeping an open mind on religious matters, even when they are in doubt.

It is just as difficult to make generalizations about professional philosophy as it is about the public perception of philosophy in general. But it is safe to say that the public perception of philosophy is correct: Philosophy is not hospitable to the supernatural. Before mentioning exceptions, it can be said that Russell's view of philosophy, based upon the assumptions of logical positivism and linguistic analysis, stands as a cipher for the attitudes and methods that created the present situation, while Adler's life and work stand for a more ancient perspective still considered largely passé.

To be fair, there have always been in the past thirty years small cadres of philosophers using the tools of positivism, analysis, and phenomenology to continue the traditional conversation between philosophy and theology. At present, the most influen-

tial among these is the so-called school of Reformed
Epistemology lead by Alvin Plantinga and Nicolas Wolterstorff.[2]
The only other significant intrusion of the supernatural into phi-
losophy has come through a revival in virtue theory lead by
Catholic convert Alasdair MacIntyre and Methodist minister
Stanley Hauerwas.[3] These two groups of philosophers have
replaced the Catholic Thomists of the 1950s as the leading
Christian intellectuals in the academy. Yet these scholars remain
isolated, working as they do in an environment that promulgates
a de facto official sanction against religious considerations.

The latest dominant intellectual trend among academics goes
by the name *postmodernism*. For all their experimentation, what
modernists had in common, like the romanticists of the previous
century, was a desire to put the pieces of civilization back together.
The modernists believed in a whole to be recovered, in a fundamental coherence and meaning to human existence that could be
retrieved. That lost whole was lying in fragments, needing only
the genius of the individual artist or thinker to reconstruct it.

Postmodernism, however, deconstructs rather than con-
structs. It rejects the belief in lost wholeness as a product of nos-
talgic bad faith. Postmodernism, as represented by the followers
of Foucault and Derrida, denies altogether the possibility of
objectivity. It posits that all knowledge is refracted through relations of class, gender, and politics. Whereas the positivist and
analytic limited the possibility of objective knowledge to the narrow criterion of verification, postmoderns give up on knowing
the object altogether.

Postmodernism assumes that selfish passions and prejudices
will always determine the content of human knowledge. Since
claims of knowledge are only veiled attempts at the exercise of
power, truth is no longer possible. Those who claim to know the
truth are merely representatives of some form of struggle of one

social class over another, one gender over another, one race over another.

Although the general sanction against the supernatural remains in effect in postmodernism, it could be argued that through postmodernism the cracks in the consensus against the supernatural are beginning to show. For example, amidst the general attack on the concept of objective truth, some philosophers working out of an existentialist background, primarily Heidegger, are aligning the postmodernism critique with the category of sin. They see the general critique of knowledge as making room for some assertion of the content of faith. The problem is that whatever content of faith is affirmed it is constantly scrutinized, subverted, it might be said, by the consciousness of sin and its effects. This is precisely the posture that a Christian post modernist wishes to strike. At the very least, they are reasserting the primacy of subjectivity in knowledge, particularly the subjective encounter of man before God.[4] The limitation of this account, in spite of its virtues, is that by accepting the premises of deconstruction these postmodern apologists remain deeply compromised by the politicized account of knowledge with which postmodernism begins.

Postmodernism, nonetheless, has reasserted the prerogatives of philosophy as a "state," or a process within the philosopher himself. In doing so, it has a tendency to reduce philosophy to nothing other than the subjective and historical conditions under which it is practiced. Since it posits that the intellect has no point of contact with the nature of things, much less with the nature of philosophy itself, postmodernism has corrected the post-Enlightenment problem with a vengeance. If the general problem with Russell's analytic approach was an ignorance of the philosopher's state, then postmodernism's corrective can be said to jettison the idea of nature altogether. In seeking to recover the philosopher's body, to speak metaphorically, they have left the specific powers of the human intellect behind.

The Philosopher's Body

Whatever minor groups exist within the academy, most professional philosophers tend to treat convictions about the supernatural as falling outside their discipline. In the popular mind, however, the supernatural has certainly not gone away. The supernatural is selling fast, on television, in film, and in bookstores. As a result, public discussion of the supernatural has been left by default to enthusiastic dilettantes. The resulting cultural phenomenon known as New Age has become the collection point for persons who instinctively seek wisdom beyond the starchy boundaries of contemporary philosophical discourse, whether couched in the cramped analytic mode or the more playful, but no less restrictive, deconstructive mode.

The success of the runaway bestseller, *Conversations with God: An Uncommon Dialogue,* by Neale Donald Walsch, with its mishmash of pop psychology and apophatic mysticism, is instructive. The shelves of large bookstores tell the tale: Metaphysics, the word coined by Aristotle for the philosophical, rational study of being, has been entirely co-opted by New Age titles. Metaphysics has come to mean eccentric speculation on religious experience and the presence of the supernatural. For anyone trained in rigorous argument, these titles rarely present a coherent narrative, and they create a great deal of confusion by their apples-are-oranges approach to speculation.

They undoubtedly speak to a need that most philosophers have long ignored, but at the cost of encouraging bad mental habits where religion, belief, and the supernatural are concerned. We need philosophers back in the business of the supernatural.

The question becomes how the philosopher can be convinced to reappropriate the subject of the supernatural for his reflection and comment. Let's assume, for argument's sake, that most philosophers relate to the supernatural, in old-fashioned Enlightenment style, as an object of reflection—one more topic to be scrutinized by reason for inclusion in an account of the world. Perhaps the philosopher can be persuaded of the possibility that the supernatural may be relevant to him in another way: important not as an object of study, but as a presence to, or influence on, the subject of philosophy, the philosopher himself. The term *subject* here refers only to the person exercising the philosophical acts; the object of that act is knowledge, which in its highest form of first principles is called wisdom.

Here we can recall Socrates once again. Before he arrived late at the banquet, recalled to us in Plato's *Symposium*, he spent hours outside listening to the promptings of his daemon. Only after submitting to these "voices" did he proceed to tell to his dinner companions the story of Diotima and her explanation of the nature of love. Socrates, in relying on the story of Diotima, doubly reinforces the lesson of his late arrival by demonstrating that he relies as much on the gift of vision as on his purely analytic gifts.

It is typical of the post-Enlightenment period to ignore this side of Socrates, his piety, and to treat him almost exclusively as the prophet of systematic skepticism and irony, rather than one who exhibited a deep piety toward the supernatural. Socrates knew he had to ready himself to philosophize, whether by making temple sacrifice or by listening to his spirit. Philosophy, as he shows through his death, requires the response of the whole person to being. Prior to postmodernism, contemporary philosophy treated itself as if it bore no relation to the state of the philosopher, in other words, as a mind without a body. Because of this, much contemporary philosophy has been reduced to ideology—even, paradoxically, postmodernism, a philosophical catechetics for the would-be politically correct.

Most people, from professional philosophers to those with a few courses under their belt, consider philosophy as a discrete body of ideas, not as a way of thinking belonging to a person. Herein lies the failure to understand that philosophy is a habitus, a deep disposition of thought, a trained habit of mind, rather than an abstract collection of principles. Philosophy, considered as merely a collection of correct conclusions, cannot admit the supernatural, especially in a secular age. Philosophy must stand separated from the supernatural and any vestiges of religious tradition, by virtue of its sole reliance on reason.

This mistake, often called rationalism or angelism, is usually identified with Rene Descartes (1596–1650), although it goes back much further into antiquity. The mistake is to represent the philosopher as solely a person of pure intelligence, and his virtues, if he has them, as irrelevant to his philosophizing. Given this view, a bad man, even a wicked man, can philosophize just as well as a good one, since the life of the mind stands apart from bodily appetite. In the older classical and medieval schema, good character offered the philosopher subjective reinforcement for his act of intelligence. Good moral habits help the mind to focus its attention on the object to be grasped. This dynamic continuity between moral and intellectual virtues makes objectivity possible. For example, a moral virtue like courage can keep prudence, an intellectual one, firmly fixed on the good to be done in the face of danger. In general, by controlling and informing the appetites, the virtues dispose the person and his highest power, intelligence, toward an object of reflection. A person lacking virtue is much more likely to err in his reasoning since his reflection may be distorted by his appetites. (The postmoderns take this distortion as an article of faith.) This argument, no doubt, is precisely the opposite of what one normally hears about the influence of religious belief on thinking.

The Philosophical Bent

By recognizing the relation between the virtues, or habits of character, one can see how philosophy can be exercised in the context of the supernatural without compromising its nature. Philosophy is nourished and fortified by this relationship, because, as Saint Thomas Aquinas puts it, grace perfects nature rather than destroying it. Supernatural grace, in this instance, comes in the form of the infused virtues of faith, hope, and charity. By these graces, the mind becomes more adept at recognizing the created order as God made it rather than projecting its own imperfections onto the world. The infused virtues dispose a person toward knowing what is other than himself, but in doing so they dispose him toward the being itself which is the gift of God, the Other. Truth itself is nothing less than the conformity of the mind to being, a conformity than can be expressed by truthful propositions. If the infused virtues encourage a person to embrace being *as a gift*, then consider the advantages of those virtues to the philosophical impulse. In addition, the highest possible object of reflection, God, is considered sacred: The person who considers truth sacred cannot but love truth to the greatest possible degree.

Intelligence is strengthened and not weakened by its reliance on supernatural grace. Grace fills the philosopher with a love for being, with a love for truth that fortifies his attention on the ultimate object of philosophy, wisdom itself. Wisdom, as the unchanging first principles that underlie all knowledge, is the final object of philosophy. Wisdom, in this sense, once known, perfects the philosophical habitus of the philosopher, just as faith, hope, and love perfect him as a person.

Descartes dreamed of the philosopher as an angel, freed from the constraints of the body, its senses and appetites. The philosopher, however, thinks with his body, through the fabric of emotions and passions that have been shaped by his personal and corporate history. Descartes falsely assumed these factors could be eliminated by a sole reliance on method, a move that over time led to the analytic and positivist assumptions that animated Bertrand Russell. As Jacques Maritain put it, Decartes denied the existence of the philosopher "as a man, asking him to lose his soul for the sake of his object. But where man departs philosophy can no longer remain."[5] Because philosophy exists in a person, and cannot be reduced to a determinate body of truths, it needs the supernatural in the form of subjective reinforcements, which are the infused virtues. To posit a connection between the character of a philosopher and the attainment of wisdom is as old as Socrates, and probably older.

Supernatural Objectivity

Prior to Descartes, philosophy benefited from its place among the theocentic humanism of the Middle Ages. Like philosophy, humanism was never the enemy of the supernatural, but rather sought to integrate itself into the picture of the larger cosmos. What was human in humanism was humanity's response to the world as given by God the Creator; unlike today, the human response was recognized as secondary. As Maritain argues, the medievals were "infatuated with objectivity" because of their devotion to a supernatural object—God.[6] The loss of objectivity began with the declaration that there was no truth above the level of reason and the natural, thus making the natural the sole terrain of philosophical reflection and unaided human reason the sole power for that reflection. Reason was deprived of not only the uplifting effect of grace but also the distinctively religious love of truth which was for centuries at the heart of Western intellectual and scientific development.

Those historians of thought who begin with secular assumptions have a difficult time explaining the sources of Western natural science in the Christian Middle Ages. What those historians do not want to recognize is precisely the point being made here: Intelligence exercised under the light of the supernatural was freed from the very prejudices and appetites that are the enemy of scientific knowledge. The case of Galileo, which is always dragged out to bash people of faith who engage in science, is not only misrepresented in itself but misrepresentative of the huge indebtedness of the natural sciences to Christian theology.[7] The tradition of theology with its confidence in cosmological order (that nature desires nothing vain), coupled with the power of the mind to discover that order through the abstraction of concepts, led to the invention of natural science out of the scholastic method. Galileo's method itself is a testimony to that theological indebtedness.

The philosopher, like the scientist, has also made use of the supernatural, probably without knowing it. The relation with the supernatural disposes the philosopher toward objectivity, but we cannot leave it at that. The supernatural also has supplied him with content through the history of revelation. The philosopher has received certain objective data from sacred traditions. Such an endowment of reason by revelation is an already established historical fact. Ideas taken from revelation (creation, the soul, God as love, and God as person) have long been utilized in Western thought. Even modern theories of personality are heavily indebted unknowingly to the doctrines of both the Incarnation and the Trinity for their metaphysical notion of the person. The basic doctrines of religion deserve to receive the philosopher's consideration since they are objects of his experience. As the historian of philosophy Etienne Gilson has shown in numerous works, these revealed data have played a decisive role in philosophical speculation even when unacknowledged.[8]

Philosophers who come to their work with positive assumptions about the supernatural are usually dismissed as prejudiced. They are accused of allowing their childhood beliefs to affect thinking that must, in Cartesian fashion, be swept clean of all assumptions. This has created an unlevel playing field: For example, anyone who imbibes the atheistic assumptions of Nietzsche from his mother's milk does not have to face the charge of delayed philosophical adolescence. The assumption of atheism, like the assumption of moral relativity, is accepted by the present philosophical community. The question, of course, is why a Nietzschean upbringing should be privileged over a Christian upbringing. The obvious, but not sole, explanation is that Nietzschean conclusions are consonant with the politically correct separation of religious belief from the moral and political consensus.

In considering the content of philosophy, one area is, arguably, crippled without the help of the supernatural—ethics. How can we know the truth about humankind without understanding either our ultimate purpose or the depth of the flaw in our nature? In fact, Maritain created a controversy when he insisted that a fully adequate ethics is impossible without the aid of the Christian concepts of sin and grace. The problem of moral philosophy in dealing with human action is that "Man is not in a state of pure nature; he is fallen and redeemed."[9] Thus, ethics, insofar as it seeks to understand humanity not in its existential being, must receive help from theology or be doomed to misunderstanding. The practical science of ethics had to understand not only the human person's nature but also the purposes for which humanity was made, a task that can only be accomplished within a supernatural context. We cannot know who we are and how we ought to act without knowing God's answers to these questions, not our own. Philosophy must be allowed to draw upon moral theology so that the principles of natural reason can be completed with the help of the supernatural. It is ironic, no doubt, that postmodernists like Westphal are returning to this basic insight although they are drawing very different conclusions.

What is controversial in Maritain's proposal is that the existential state of humanity, the historical and the particular, should exceed the reach of philosophy and require the aid of theology. Indeed, Maritain insisted from his earliest writings that the philosophy of Saint Thomas Aquinas was more existential than existentialism. Modern intelligence, in proudly rejecting the supernatural, finds itself paradoxically out of touch with humankind's finitude. And the paradoxes sadly multiply: Cartesian skepticism originally began as questioning any truth above reason itself. What Descartes sought explicitly to avoid, the authority of the sensate, has come to pass because the mind has lost confidence in its judgments. History shows that the supernatural, working through personal faith and historical tradition, strengthens intelligence in its own order.

This example of Descartes, however, serves to demonstrate what is lost by divorcing the philosopher and the supernatural. Philosophy, as a result, knows less about the humanity it wants so desperately to understand before anything else. Even further, philosophy, which encourages a perfection of mental habits, actually encourages the atrophy of intelligence itself. The mind is naturally inclined toward being, and when it is cut off or shut in upon itself, the mind withers and dies like a tree deprived of the light. Philosophy needs the supernatural so that intelligence is renewed in its natural love for being. The supernatural helps to restore reason, without which the habit of philosophy cannot develop.

Returning the supernatural to philosophy is a project that calls for intellectual and spiritual boldness. Regardless of the state of philosophy, there can be no compromise with the present age. As Maritain wrote in the 1930s, "Modern civilization is a worn-out garment. One cannot sew new pieces on it. It requires total and, may I say, substantial recasting, a transvaluation of cultural principles."[10] Only a supernatural, evangelical consciousness wedded to philosophy, belonging to the philosopher living in faith, will be unafraid of challenging the false intellectual currency of the day and will begin to effect the true renewal of the mind and the recovery of the body.

NOTES:

1   John H. Hick, *The Existence of God*, (Old Tappan, NJ: MacMillan Publishing Company, 1964).

2   Alvin Plantinga and Nicolas Wolterstorff, eds., *Faith and Rationality: Reason and Belief in God* (Notre Dame, IN: University of Notre Dame Press, 1984).

3   Alasdair MacIntyre, *After Virtue: A Study in Moral Theory*, 2nd ed. (Notre Dame, IN: University of Notre Dame Press, 1984); Stanley Hauerwas, *Vision and Virtue: Essays in Christian Ethical Reflection*, (Notre Dame, IN: University of Notre Dame Press, 1981).

4   Merold Westphal, "Taking St. Paul Seriously: Sin as an Epistemological Category," in *Christian Philosophy*, ed. Thomas P. Flint (Notre Dame, IN: University of Notre Dame Press, 1991), 200-226.

5   Jacques Maritain, *An Essay on Christian Philosophy*, trans. Edward H. Flannery (New York: Philosophical Library, 1955), 16.

6   Ibid., 46-47.

7   See Stanley Jaki, *The Road of Science and the Ways to God* (Chicago: University of Chicago Press, 1978).

8   Etienne Gilson, *Christianity and Philosophy*, trans. Ralph McDonald, C.S.B. (New York: Sheed & Ward, 1939).

9   Maritain, *Essay on Christian Philosophy*, 39.

10 *Integral Humanism: Temporal and Spiritual Problems of a New Christendom*, trans. Joseph W. Evans (New York: Charles Scribner's Sons, 1973), 207.

REVELATIONS

SUSAN BERGMAN

HIDDEN SIGHTS

THE CONVINCINGNESS
OF UNREASONED EXPERIENCE

Daniel answered before the king and said, "as for the mystery about which the King has inquired, neither wise men, conjurers, magicians, nor diviners are able to declare it to the king. However, there is a God in heaven who reveals mysteries."

—Daniel 2:27-28a

BY THE TIME JESUS CALLED HIS FRIEND LAZARUS back to life, he was drawing both faithful and skeptical followers wherever he traveled. He had given twelve of his followers power over all the demons and power to heal diseases, and then he sent seventy-two more ahead of him to towns he was about to enter, announcing the nearness of the kingdom of God. Luke speaks of this time as one in which Jesus rejoiced in the fullness of the Spirit. "I praise Thee, O Father, Lord of heaven and earth," Luke quotes Jesus as saying, "that Thou didst hide these things from the wise and intelligent and didst reveal them to babes." (Luke 10:21). Then turning to his disciples he said, "Blessed are the eyes which see the things you see, for I say to you, that many prophets and kings wished to see the things which you see, and did not see them, and to hear the things which you hear, and did not hear them" (Luke 10:23b–24). The evidence of God's presence—in miracles, in resurrection, in the supernatural causes within natural phenomena—however manifold, will never be proof enough for some. They will see water turned into wine before their very eyes, but will be blind to the significance of what has happened. There are two kinds of sight that Jesus is talking about: physical and spiritual, the sight of the eyes and the sight of the heart. The one is common to all who look, the other must be revealed.

What William James, in his lecture "The Reality of the Unseen," calls the "convincingness of unreasoned experience" depends less on rational explanations than on the one experiencing. "The unreasoned and immediate assurance is the deep thing in us, the reasoned argument is but a surface exhibition. Instinct leads, intelligence does but follow."[1] While the evidence of God's hand in the ordinary may be obvious, sometimes overwhelming, if we are to experience even a small part of the revelation that filled Jesus with such joy, we must be given eyes of faith and a disposition to *see*.

In Jesus' time, as now, so many wanted to experience a convincing sign. What were these hidden things Jesus spoke of that kings and prophets were denied? They sat for hours waiting to find out. They attended his talks religiously. "Give us a sign from Heaven," some said. One woman, evidently overcome with profound feeling, called out from the crowd, "Blessed is the womb that bore You, and the breasts at which You nursed" (Luke 11:27b). The crowd must have turned toward the woman, attentively, must have sensed the urgency of her insight: They were not accustomed to hearing from women about matters of the body in public gatherings. I imagine others around her beginning, with soft affection in their voices, to bless the mother of Jesus. Though at the time it is improbable that the crowd had any awareness of the virgin birth, let alone its significance as a fulfillment of Isaiah's prophecy or its demonstration of Christ's divinity, the woman recognized in the image of the mother something fleshy yet pure. But Jesus seems to have known that the woman had already become fixated on an earthly episode, a sign, which endangered her fuller understanding. He stops her from her well-intentioned homage to his mother, shifting her attention to his heavenly Father saying, "On the contrary, blessed are those who hear the word of God and observe it" (Luke 11:28).

In addressing her I think Jesus is alluding to the difference between walking by sight and walking by faith. Maybe at that moment the veils disintegrated that covered the eyes of her heart, and she saw more clearly. I suspect, however, that the truth Jesus had said was revealed to babes, was hidden from her a while longer, while she sulked and clung to what she could see of this world. I understand this tempation to claim for a sign the place of what the sign points to, to crave its power to convince, rather than to unreasonably, sometimes even blindly, trust and obey the Word.

Compare this admonition to the words Jesus speaks when he meets up with the disciples he has sent ahead of him, whom he finds marveling at the power they have seen manifest through their own acts. He says to them, "I saw Satan fall like lightning from heaven. I have given you authority to trample on snakes and scorpions and to overcome all the power of the enemy; nothing will harm you. *However, do not rejoice that the spirits submit to you, but rejoice that your names are written in heaven"* (Luke 10:17–20 NIV). He responds to their accounts of miraculous deeds: Yes, you are defeating the enemy, but don't rejoice that you are agents of the supernatural; rather, rejoice that you are children of the heavenly Father.

Jesus knows us all too well. His words to both the woman and his disciples repeat the same caution. Be careful, he urges, to see what is revealed to you through the eyes of your faith. The visible world, the magnificent, tangible experience, is a shadow of, a pointer to, the heavenly world to come. If the scorpion trampling and the spirit handling were the thing, we would devote ourselves to the show, Jesus understood, ranking each other in order of demonstrable signs and wonders, and we would miss the invisible God.

Yet, while urging transcendent sight, Jesus does not do away with the sign. He himself introduces the image of Satan falling from heaven. It was God who decided to convey his son into the world through the womb of a virgin. It is the story of a baby in a manger we tell more than any other to point toward an incarnation we do not fully understand. The iconoclast would sweep the house of any image in order to prevent the unsuspecting from falling under the sway of the visible world. The overzealous reformer would deny to the Body of Christ contemporary manifestations of certain spiritual gifts and miracles, in fear that they will eclipse the giver of the gift. Instead, what if, given a spirit of power, of love, and of a sound mind, we were able to accept Jesus' teaching that some people would be given to see and from others the same knowledge would be hidden? "We understand nothing of the works of God, if we do not take as a principle that he has willed to blind some, and enlighten others," writes Pascal about the hiddenness of God. We see in part: That to which one person is blind is revealed to another. What if we were to think of this not as an impairment, but as a truth that binds us into a humble participation in the community of the kingdom of God?

I think it is for this experience of seeing what God reveals of himself through others that we are encouraged to come into regular fellowship with a body of believers: "Let us consider how to stimulate one another to love and good deeds, not forsaking our own assembling together, as is the habit of some, but encouraging one another; and all the more, as you see the day [of Christ's return] drawing near" (Heb. 10:24–25). We assemble so that the variegated threads of the glory of God can take form visibly, not in the one life, but in the many. The challenge I have experienced again and again, as I enter into community with others who share faith in Christ, is to receive gratefully the particular knowledge revealed to me, however modest or perplexing, and to offer this freely to others, while at the same time accepting freely from others, without judgment or envy, what they have been given. More often one showing is treasured and another is scrapped, if its presence is recognized at all.

After my freshman year in college I spent the summer living in the red-light district in Amsterdam, in a youth hostel where I helped make beds and mop floors. I was part of a student mission program sponsored by my college. Some of us traveled around Europe taking the good news of salvation with us; some stayed in one place. It had fallen to me that every other day I had dinner shift at the Shelter, which meant, because of our efficiently limited menu, that I prepared ham and cheese omelets on toast for the hostel guests. They sat at the counter, having arrived with little money from places such as Paris, or Rome, or Egypt, and we talked together about where we came from in the world. Some told of their distant families; some spoke of displacement or exile. Some drifted in from Vandal Square so high on drugs they seemed to devour their food without breathing. I was there to tell them about the love of Jesus, and when they asked why I was there, I did.

The staff and student volunteers at the hostel began the day with a Bible study and prayer time led by a woman called Truus, the director of the student program there. I grew quickly to love her. She taught me a few Dutch phrases, laughing good-naturedly at my faltering pronunciation. She kept an eye on me when the Italian boys came around with their guitars, and one weekend, she drove with me to the coast of the North Sea for what she described as a time of intensive prayer. The way I prayed was fine, she said, but her kind of prayer went further than her head. She could simply invite the Holy Spirit to come and pray for her, and the words began, in a mellifluous utterance, reserved for God alone, to spill from her being.

She was an extrovert, wild with praise, her arms freely lifted to the heavens. All day she would sing little choruses of joy while I tried not to mope about, struggling with my poverty, my noisy, cheerleader-of-a-mission teammate from the States, probably struggling with homesickness. Truus also led a Bible study, one day a week, for the prostitutes in our neighborhood. She took oranges and Mars bars to their children. I had seen her try to cast a demon, in the name of Jesus, from a strung-out, raging hulk of a man who forced his way into the hostel at midnight demanding money and a needle. She placed her hand on him, spoke an authoritative prayer, and he fell to his knees by the front desk, temporarily sedated. I wanted to be exactly like she was: spiritually complete, worker of miracles, picture of the woman who knows the heart of God. So when I watched the sun drape itself over the water as we walked along the deserted beach, I soaked in every word she said. We stopped when we had passed the row of striped cabanas and knelt in the cool sand, and she laid her hands on my head. Fervently, she invited the Spirit of God to give me the supernatural gift of tongues, so that I might be blessed with a deeper prayer. "We are waiting on you, Lord," she said patiently.

This was the second such request that summer. Once before, a team of Truus's friends, who manifested what I understood to be a richer set of spiritual gifts than mine, had placed their hands on my head and petitioned God on my behalf. They crowded around, all asking for the same fullness to fill me, fully believing. I must not have been ready, Truus said, though I know others must have thought of me as stubborn or unworthy. Maybe I needed to be alone, less distracted. Maybe I possessed a deep root of rebellion whose tendrils needed to be wrenched from the hard flesh of my heart. This is completely possible, if not likely. On the beach she spoke words over me that were not in any language familiar to either of us. Her tone was pleading. She pressed her fingers tenderly along the sides of my temples. I opened my mouth, truly willing. "Dear God," I said, "examine my heart. Please don't let me miss the gifts you have for me by any sort of resistance or constraint, or sin on my part." I said something like that, hoping the words would suddenly transform themselves into sounds like the ones I had heard released from the mouths of the Christians in Amsterdam, and not the cerebral ascent that left some willful root tangled around my heart. I said that prayer and nothing more. We waited in the music of Truus's faithful prayers until the sun had slipped below the line where the sea curved. And then we walked back to her car.

I know I disappointed her. We spent an awkward evening eating at an inexpensive Vietnamese restaurant. At home in her tiny apartment before bed she served me a cup of the liquidy yellow pudding they called flan. She had made a bed for me out of blankets on the floor and let me have her pillow. I remember her asking God to double our sleep that night so that we would wake refreshed. She must have been exhausted. I have often wondered if her prayer could have been answered yes, as well, if I had somehow gotten my mind out of the way.

It is almost twenty years later, and a woman at the bakery tells me she buried a plastic statue of St. Joseph upside down behind the house she wanted to sell. She did not really count on St. Joseph to produce a buyer, but friends had told her of this method's success and what if it worked? Days after she had taken her trowel and dug up a small divot of grass, tucking the figure in, as she did her children at night, two legitimate offers materialized within hours of the other.

Julian of Norwich, in the late fourteenth century, came on three truths of God as she contemplated a hazelnut lying in the palm of her hand. She writes:

> I looked at it and thought: What can this be? And I was given this general answer: It is everything which is made. I was amazed that it could last, for I thought that it was so little that it could suddenly fall into nothing. And I was answered in my understanding: It lasts and always will, because God loves it; and thus everything has being through the love of God.
>
> In this little thing I saw three properties. The first is that God made it, the second is that he loves it, the third is that God preserves it. But what is that to me?

It is that God is the Creator and the lover and the protector.[2]

A writer friend phoned to tell me of her bargain with God. She would write an essay on Archbishop Oscar Romero if, when she prayed to God to help her, she found the wedding ring she had lost. She did not exactly have the time to spare. This seemed like an unlikely enough outcome, in her mind, to release her from yet another obligation. A month had passed, and no sign of the treasured gold band had appeared. She struck the bargain, unexpectantly. That day, or maybe the next, she saw the ring shining in the grass near the left tire of her car when she parked in her driveway. How had it gotten there? She was calling me to say the essay was almost complete. In praying for her ring to appear she had not anticipated the recovery of a taped interview, lost for seventeen years, which she had recorded with Romero, the last interview he gave before he died.

An unchurched boy in the stands at a baseball game felt an urge to pray for the batter, his favorite player, at full count. "Dear God, if you're there," the boy began, "please let Ryne hit at least a single." It was that home run, after the boy's prayer, I am told by a neighbor, that brought the boy to faith in God.

Was no one praying for the pitcher? I want to ask.

It is not the sign alone that is important, I am reminded again, but accepting what was once hidden that we are suddenly given to see.

Describing what she takes to be an ordinary miracle, Frederica Mathewes-Green writes of her pilgrimage to the Eastern Orthodox Church of St. George in the Chicago suburb of Cicero. She wanted to witness a wooden icon of the *Theotokos,* the Virgin Mary, that had been weeping since the Friday evening before Holy Week, April 1994. "The tears are oily in substance and leave a double shiny trail down the Virgin's red robe and over the hand of her son, which is raised in blessing. Even when, as now, the episodes of weeping are less frequent, the visible trail of tears remains," she testifies. And then, because she has come to expect no less than the visible presence of God in our worship of him, she continues, "Of course, conversions and healings have followed in its wake, as people were anointed with the tears."[3]

I look around me at the broad and free-wheeling faith of those I admire. Comparatively, my experience of the supernatural pales, I am tempted to think. Where are my signs and wonders? I have not seen the Virgin weep, though I have watched my mother, with a sorrow deeper than any I have known, consoled by the mercy and comfort of God. In her smile God's glory begins to show. Nor can I imagine seeing all that Julian did in the round globe of a hazelnut. I am concentrating on the words of the chorus we are singing at my sister's church, when the man standing beside me falls into the aisle smitten with holy laughter. He rolls around the cramped space in what strikes me as a rather hideous bliss. For me God appears in moments of quiet recognition: a word or a phrase that strikes me to the core, as a still, small voice once outdid a rushing wind. "Somehow I have to trust that God is at work in me and that the way I am being moved to new inner and outer places is part of a larger movement of which I am only a very small part," writes Henri Nouwen.[4]

To acknowledge that one is a very small part of something much larger than one's self is to be able to celebrate the potential wholeness of God's revelation without despairing of one's own limits, or of another's. It is to celebrate the kingdom of God, as Jesus did, among the sick and blind and lost. It is helpful to recognize that a small part has a limited view and particular gifts, and that the whole will shape the part, just as the part will alter, perhaps enhance, the whole. The Australian writer David Malouf, in his novel *Remembering Babylon*, beautifully describes the unique contribution of the individual showing forth God, in the character of the Parson whose wife of thirty-three years understands him better than he does himself. "Cleverness, she knows, has nothing to do with what he is after; which is revelation. What will be revealed, he believes, is the unique gift that is in each man and woman, in each creature and plant too—what else has his study of nature shown him?—and must also be in him: a gift he alone can give to the world, and which without him it must lack."[5]

In the past several years I have witnessed these unique, God-revealing gifts as I have participated in the liturgical arts group at the church I attend. The sheer array of different skill sets and personalities visible among this small group within a local church strikes me as one of the more beautiful evidences of God's handiwork. There, on any given project, one designs, one drafts to scale, one chooses the perfect color, several construct or sew, others paint, write, dance, administrate. At the end of one person's abilities and service, another's begins, until the work of the church is completed.

My job has been to design, and then to select and assemble the cloths and braids we use for our fabric hangings. These are the jobs I most want and others seem to avoid. They marvel at the way patterns and textures blend that they might have found unsuitable together, as I marvel at the perfect construction of the frame that one of our carpenters has assembled. Each individual, if in the right place, enjoys his or her job the most, to all of our amazement, and feels affirmed for doing what he or she does best. When I have approached the quilting table, though I am welcome, I have found the experts there mildly fretting over my imperfect stitches and graciously urging me to enjoy a cup of tea to keep my hands otherwise employed while I visit with them. The result of offering, in return to God and to each other, the gifts with which he has uniquely equipped each member of the body, not only pictures, but lets us experience, God's kingdom.

In my everyday work as a writer, however, I have a little more trouble keeping in touch with that kind of revelation—the experiencing of the presence of God that comes through fellowship. My own limits encroach. Like most writers I know, I have not yet learned to balance concentrated time alone, which the craft requires, with community life. Certainly the kingdom of God is just as present in the world, but by the end of a long project, I often feel as if I have wandered off into a sort of dark, endless cave alone. Presently I am working to complete a job, which, though small, has already taken me four years. I am writing a book that frequently strikes me as a job more suited to a stronger, wiser person, someone to whom things are generally less hidden, with fewer children, and a disposition less melancholy, a job that I cannot possibly complete without the intervention and sustenance of God himself. And that's the point, isn't it?—I tell myself—to glimpse in what we ordinarily see and touch, the extraordinary that we have not yet seen.

But the story is dark and difficult, and, as is common with stories that are true, people along the way prefer that it not be told. Who knows what complex of reasons compelled me to enter the deep trouble of other people's lives? There were blatantly conflicting accounts of the same events, and a cast of dozens as families divided and collapsed. As a writer I as intrigued by the story. I thought by telling it I could help, and I waded in.

From city to city as my research began, I came across remarkably similar tales of early childhood brutality with little variation, stories remembered, suddenly, in a counselor's office or in a hospital ward. Therapists talked in hushed confidences about clients with Multiple Personality Disorder, clients who were suicidal, whose allegedly abusive families they had urged their clients to disavow. In courtrooms and treatment centers, in police interviews and lawyers' offices, in advanced training sessions for therapists, and in clinics where women huddled in locked corridors, I began to see a pattern in the process by which these "memories" were being generated and sustained. Hypnosis, guided imagery, sand trays, sodium amytal, a literalistic rather than a symbolic interpretation of dreams were the techniques used. Bewilderingly, not a single person involved in trying to help these alleged victims had checked the accuracy or possible inaccuracy of the wilder and wilder claims that were ruining the lives of these supposed victims and their families.

My therapist friends wondered what issues this project was bringing up for me. They begged me, for my safety, not to get involved. Regardless of the truth of the claims, the well-meaning counselors assured me, they were going to treat their clients' pain. I should think of my family. Couldn't I write a book about happiness?

Early in my research, a therapist I knew as a friend, whom I will call Joey, told me about a woman who did not believe her "memories" at first. Often they were too horrible to believe. She had to be put in a survivors' group before she would be convinced that her symptoms indicated what her doctors said they did. Her father was not a monster, she insisted. But eventually, once she had been checked into the hospital ward, her prescription dosages adjusted, once she had undergone a sodium amytal interview, and had it played back for her, she did believe them. They knew what they were doing, she came to realize. Why hadn't she seen it before?

When Joey told me about her, it was not the first case of

recovered memories I had heard. With the fervor of new converts, women of my generation were entering therapy with a troubled sense of self, crumbling marriages, postpartum depression, anger issues; just at the moment in history when we were most free to choose for ourselves, they were giving away their lives. What was causing this disabling form of self-reinvention? The boredom endemic to the suburbs? Blame for the consequences of our choices that we could not bear to place on ourselves? I wanted to find out. Raising questions, needless to say, alienated many of the people who were generous enough to spend time with me. At some level we all wanted the same things, didn't we? We wanted to help. But given the same devastating signs and symptoms, we were not given to see the same things. After Joey's initial helpfulness with information and introductions within his professional circle, he and I did not speak much, except in passing, for about two years. He was blindly coaching false memory, as I had reluctantly come to understand it. I ached for the needy in his care. In his mind I must have been conducting my own misguided moral crusade.

Meanwhile neurologists published their studies on the suggestibility of memory. Psychiatrists and psychologists began an internal critique of their methods and results. The notion of repression itself, avowed and disavowed by Freud, came under scrutiny in many camps. The media kicked in with its sensationalized coverage. Courts reversed decisions that had held the innocent in prison. Back at home in my third-floor study, I spent months and months trying to craft, from among the ruins, a novel that would help make sense of this story of our time.

The week I was to mail a draft of the book to my publisher, a few friends offered to pray with me before I sent the project out into the world. They asked for God's protection in my family's life against the controversy the story would generate. They thanked God for his strength that enabled me to continue the work. They asked for God's intervention and healing, and restoration among families, and deliverance from fear, and for peace to come among those who saw the issues differently. We prayed for wisdom, and I think someone might have prayed for good reviews.

It was the Sunday after that prayer that I saw Joey at a local craft fair. He walked over and stood by me while our children glued Popsicle stick cabins together. He started talking about hunting, and children, and music, easily, as if months had not passed between us in silence. His standing there I took to be God's direct answer to someone's prayers, maybe mine. Joey had cleared the air, and then I told him that I had sent in my novel that week.

"You're sort of in it," I said, unsure of what I would say next. "Part of you is part of a character you might recognize. The fictionalized version of you played the guitar in college, like you did." Joey was chewing on the inside of his cheek. I kept talking. "In the novel he's a therapist named Joey. He has a client with memories of abuse who kills herself."

"You must be thinking of the woman in the hospital," he said.

"Before the book is published I wanted to talk with you. I know we didn't exactly agree when we last talked." I was worried. I thought that the publication of the novel would continue to deepen the rift between us. Though he was only a fragment of a wonderful character, our mutual friends who read the book would not see it that way. I would be relegated to my cave, again. But then something happened that I could not have imagined until I heard him say what he did.

"Oh Susan," Joey said, shaking his head slowly. "I was so lost." I think I must have gulped for air. "We completely misread the signs," he said. "But now I'm found. You can't imagine how terrified I was, how deep I'd gotten into believing that whole thing. Every day we feared for our lives. Our clients would come in with threats from imaginary occult operatives whom we all believed had abused them. My partner was sleeping in the hallway in front of his children's bedroom at night." The worst of it was that their clients became sicker and more lost. They had had to overhaul their approach to therapy completely, he said. "We don't go back and back and dig around, when a client comes in. We talk about today. I'm not sure now if any of it ever happened." He had wanted to be a hero, was how he put it. "Whatever you write about me, during that dark period, and more, would be true. The story needs to be told. I'm honored you put me in your book."

For a minute there, amazed though I was, I was also Jonah sitting under her vine wondering how in the world he had had such a remarkable change of heart. When God hid something from the likes of kings and prophets wasn't it because they were incapable of being convinced? The reality of the unseen is indeed unreasonable not to depend at all, for its appearance, on the subject's deserving. And what about the years his clients had lost and their families—would those lives and relationships ever possibly be restored? And had not I come all this way bearing this heavy story, through what felt like the belly of a great fish—that one sign of Jonah that Jesus said he would give to an unbelieving and perverse generation? Here I was in my ordinary life and the hand of God, powerful to save, had suddenly materialized.

It had happened again: I had done the work in front of me, day after day, alone, so that I had lost sight of the big picture. Yet, in one peculiar miracle, I was reminded of my small part in the larger body of Christ: I was given a sense of confirmation in my individual work, and at the same time I recognized the vast, eternal nearness of the Kingdom of heaven. Where I least expected to sense the presence of God, when I finally picked up my head, lately so buried in the stack of papers on my desk, there he was, having already transformed lives, committed acts of deliverance and justice, defeated the enemy. Had I thought I was the only one to whom he would show mercy? I recovered enough to put my hand out to shake Joey's and he embraced me, warmly. *I was lost and now am found*, he had said, which is exactly what God does for me, every day, for each of us uniquely: the hiding and the showing.

NOTES

1 William James, *Varieties of Religious Experience* (New York: Random House, 1902), 73.

2 *Julian of Norwich, "Showings,"* trans. Edmund Colledge and James Walsh (Mahwah, NJ: Paulist Press, 1978), 130-31.

3 Frederica Mathewes-Green, *Facing East: A Pilgrim's Journey into the Mysteries of Orthodoxy* (San Francisco: Harper San Francisco, 1997), 151.

4 Henri J. M. Nouwen, *In the Name of Jesus* (New York: Crossroad, 1989), 9.

5 David Malouf, *Remembering Babylon* (New York: Random House, 1994), 135.

PAUL
MARIANI

THE WORD
AS LIVING FLAME

BECAUSE I AM AN ENTHUSIAST in the root sense of the word, and because I tend toward the Romantic side of things, I am going to approach the topic of divine inspiration in the Bible as coolheadedly as possible to see what light I can shed on what happens when I read the Scriptures, especially the Gospels. I have been writing poems and biographies long enough to know that what I do—even with hard work and occasional inspiration—and what the Gospel narratives do to me when I approach them are two quite different things. In fact, the Gospels—I mean the canonical Gospels (Matthew, Mark, Luke, John), not Thomas or Peter or Jude or the apocryphal texts, pious as they are—seem to me *sui generis*, unduplicable. Reading them, one senses that one is in the presence of an inspired text. This sense marks the Gospels as authentic and the other texts as uninspired, derivative.

In truth the Gospels are like no other work I know, different even from the Hebrew Scriptures, or Paul's epistles, or Revelation, all of them likewise inspired by the spirit of God. Perhaps this is because the Gospels are closer to Ground Zero, the Incarnational moment itself. Only Acts, Luke's Book II, carries over some of the narrative power of his Gospel, a ripple unfolding in the wake of Christ's life. It is sometimes called the Gospel of the Holy Spirit, taking its power from the life of Christ as that was transformed into the life of the early Christian Church, Christ's second body, if you will.

For forty years now I have been reading the Scriptures, at times distractedly, at times so intently that I have found myself writing out the words so that I could try to hear them more deeply in the physical act of writing. And always—when I have been able to give the words something of the attention and reverence they deserve—I come away refreshed and amazed. They are words I have read and reread hundreds of times, but because I believe they are also words by which God is speaking to me, they somehow remain—to borrow a phrase Ezra Pound used to describe poetry—news that really does stay news.

I know that my own work as a poet and a biographer, not to say as a teacher, has been profoundly shaped by my reading of the Bible, as well as by Biblical commentary, homiletics, even the words of others when I detect they have been irradiated by the Bible. How often I have stolen from the Bible, calling it inspiration: the Muse of poetry doffing her hat in the direction of the Spirit. I know too that my own work has been both consciously and unconsciously affected by my reading of the Scriptures, in ways beyond my ability to detect. In truth, each of the biographies I have written—Gerard Manley Hopkins, William Carlos Williams, John Berryman, Robert Lowell, Hart Crane—has been shaped by my search for the inner spiritual life which also shaped each of these poets in turn. Regardless of how their journeys seemed to end—in affirmation or despair—their eyes remained focused on the light as they had come to understand that light.

The truth is that part of my search for the spiritual core in others, and the forms that spirituality takes, stems from my belief in the underlying authority and mind-dazzling significance of the implications (and complications) of the Incarnation. By the Incarnation I mean God's entrance into the world of time and materiality not only in his words but even more intimately in his Word, Christ, *Ipse*, Son. It is a fact which by its very nature must necessarily have changed forever all human activity, raising it to a higher level, and giving all we do a radically new significance because the divine has entered the equation.

It is as if, because God had become human, when Christ later was raised on the cross, he raised us with him, intersecting our horizontal realm so that our lives forever after (and, by extension, before as well) came into intimate contact with the vertical realm of the Godhead. Call it God's finger underwriting all we do and giving to it an inestimable value, not because of anything we merited, but because God made it and saw that what he had done was good. It means that the Creator of the universe, with all its expanding galaxies and black holes and quarks and particles and ions and anti-matter and matter, entered into the womb of human creation via a young Jewish woman from the hill town of Nazareth, thus altering step by incredible step the course and direction of human history forever after.

Several years ago, a friend of mine, a well-known poet, remarked how terrific it would have been if Norman Mailer had been around in the first century to do a kind of new journalistic reading of Jesus, following Jesus around and reporting on him the way, say, he had reported on the 1968 Republican convention in Miami. Ironically, as it turned out, Mailer obliged by showing us the dismal results of such a reading in his *Gospel According to the Son.* "I feel your pain," Mailer has Jesus say at one point, and the inevitable image of Bill Clinton at a fundraiser immediately springs to mind. At other times Mailer has the Nazarene talking like some parody of Jewish Confucianism.

No, the "You Are There" approach, it appears, will not do anything like the job the Gospels have done. I have read John Dominic Crossan and the other results of the Jesus Seminar sufficiently to realize the hopelessness of ever recovering the historic Jesus. Besides, we are not looking for an historical individual—the very idea of recovering the historical Jesus was an invention of nineteenth-century German Higher Criticism—and we know that reporting on anyone depends as much on who is reporting and on what is being reported as it does on the actual events. We also know enough about human subjectivity to realize there could never be an "exact" description of the figure of Jesus, even if we were standing before him. "Who do people say I am?" Jesus asks at one point, and the answer comes back. Some say one thing, some another. To which Jesus replies, "But who do you say I am?" Has the question or the answer changed, really, in the past two thousand years?

Besides, something far more important is taking place in the Gospels, which were never meant to be biographies in the first place. Actually, they are more like God's poems, multi-layered, rich, and enriching. How many monks, desert fathers (and mothers), and saints have been transformed by a single sentence lifted from the Bible, read as a direct summons to them to go and do likewise? How many millions of people have turned to the Bible, asking the Word of God to speak to them, comfort them, guide them, transform them? Here, picked at random, are words for the mass for November 10, which remembers St. Leo the

Great, pope and doctor of the Church. From the Book of Wisdom: "Let honesty prompt your thinking about the Lord, seek him in simplicity of heart." From Psalm 139, read at the Responsorial:

> O LORD, you have probed me and you know me;
> you know when I sit and when I stand;
> you understand my thoughts from afar.

Or the Gospel Acclamation, from the first letter of John, reminding us that "Whoever keeps the word of Christ grows perfect in the love of God."

Any one of those, taken seriously, could serve as the theme of an entire retreat, in truth an entire life, and never be emptied or exhausted. I have followed some version of the *lectio divina* or the Ignatian *Spiritual Exercises* long enough to realize that the composition of place is neither an exact science nor an end in itself. For always the evoked scene points back to oneself and to where that self is on the journey. It is also true, however, that the Lord waits always in the midst, no matter how far we travel, no matter if we pass through war, rumors of war, night alarms, tedium, exhaustion, trials by fire, by drought, by plague, by locust or other hungry insect, by hunger, by temptation. But we also experience joy, jubilation, exultation, quiet, comfort, succor, the voice of God in the whispering wind.

So it is with the Gospel stories. For, regardless of where you pick them up, they work on you. To read them as literature or as a story or even as a moral lesson is to miss the point. They are still spiritually radioactive enough, however, that they are going to work on you if you give them the least chance to do so. It is as if, when you read them, they read you back. But it is the nature of God's Word to bear fruit in us. It is always an invitation, graciously offered. And since it is an invitation, we are always free to accept it or not.

Consider the story of Zacchaeus (Luke 19:1–10), a man of some not insignificant power in the ancient crossroads city of Jericho, a tax collector, a Jew despised by his fellow Jews for doing the work of the hated Roman government, a runt of a man, but with enough ingenuity to climb a sycamore in order to catch a glimpse of Jesus as he passes by. So, when Jesus recognizes him and calls him by name and tells him he will have supper at his house, the crowd is astonished. How can this holy man dine with a sinner?

But Zacchaeus, ecstatic that Jesus has called him—and his response to that call has transformed him on the spot—holds his ground. He means to change, he says, and to prove it he publicly announces before the crowd—who no doubt will hold him to his word—what he plans to do. "Look, sir," he says, his tiny frame standing firm, "I am going to give half my property to the poor, and if I have cheated anybody I will pay him back four times the amount," in other words the highest amount prescribed by Jewish and Roman law.

And Jesus? "Today salvation has come to this house"—at once, now, and not only to Zacchaeus but to his entire household—"because this man too is a son of Abraham," a Jew in the full sense of the word, one who hungers after justice and righteousness. After all, Jesus adds, "the Son of Man has come to seek out and save what was lost." And now Jesus faces west toward Jerusalem, prepared—though he does not say so—to give everything, including his own life, to do just that: to seek out and save what was lost.

Consider the vexing question of inspiration. Milton seems to have found a way into the Scriptures that he could turn to good use for his poetry. It was a case of inspiration leading to inspiration. It is as if in *Paradise Lost* he was on a mission from God, God's advocate as it were, sent to justify God's ways toward man. Nightly the lines came to him unbidden, lines which he then transcribed to the page. "Sing, heavenly Muse," he wrote, invoking Urania, the Muse of the highest vision available to humankind (a Muse in whom he did not believe but whom he invoked because it was the accepted mode of those steeped in the classics). But he also insisted on invoking the Holy Spirit, in whom he most certainly did believe:

> Sing, heavenly Muse, that on the secret top
> Of Oreb, or of Sinai, didst inspire
> That shepherd who first taught the chosen seed
> In the beginning how the heavens and earth
> Rose out of Chaos; or if Sion hill
> Delight thee more, and Siloa's brook that flowed
> Fast by the oracle of God, I thence
> Invoke thy aid to my adventurous song,
> That with no middle flight intends to soar
> Above the Aeonian mount, while it pursues
> Things unattempted yet in prose or rhyme.

Come, oh selfsame spirit who inspired Moses on the sacred mountain, Milton begins his epic invocation, that same Spirit who gave the law to Moses and inspired him, as Milton believed, to compose the first five books of the Bible, including Genesis (which Milton would now rewrite in his own epic poem, and with his own glossings). Or if the Spirit should now reside in the holy city of Jerusalem (Sion hill and Siloa's brook), then he will address the Spirit there. In any event, he means to go beyond Mount Helicon, by which he means the muse of classical antiquity, to attempt what has not been attempted before, except perhaps by Father Moses. And for that ascent he will need nothing short of the Holy Spirit.

As a poet I have often thought of Milton—most often with chagrin, of course—as I have tried to find a way to channel the energy, say, of the Psalms, into my own poems. Have I been able to do that? I do not know, though I may favor four- and five-line stanzus because I have spoken or prayed the Responsorial Psalms along with the congregation for the past half century. Closer to my own experience, I think, is that of Father Hopkins, who attempted his own modest justification of God's ways toward men in his *Wreck of the Deutschland*, by trying to explain why bad things happen to good people. In this instance it was the death by drowning of five Franciscan nuns (along with fifty others) in a winter storm in the mouth of the Thames River in December 1875. Like Milton, he too called upon the Spirit to help him understand what the event meant from God's perspective: "Breathe, arch and original Breath."

I believe I have been blessed in my own way, for there have been moments when true inspiration (I have to believe) came to me unbidden while reading the Scriptures. Once it was the powerful and desolate Psalm 88, when I recalled something I'd experienced in the holding cell in the basement of the high priest Caiaphas's palace. The cell—fifteen feet deep, perhaps—had originally been a cistern, but it had cracked in the first century before Christ and inevitably gone dry, becoming in turn a place for holding prisoners overnight. Very likely one of the prisoners held there, following the agony in the garden and being taken prisoner, was Jesus himself. The Romans under Titus would burn Caiaphas's place to the ground as they inched their way up the slopes of Jerusalem in AD 70. Centuries later the church of St. Peter of the Cockcrow would be constructed over the old foundations. Several years ago, standing at the bottom of the cistern with a group of pilgrims, listening to a Franciscan priest read Psalm 88, I would write "The Cistern," quoting from the psalm.

Another poem came from a meditation on a passage from Isaiah, about the foolishness of trying to flee from God. It was a passage handed to me on a slip of paper by a Jesuit who was conducting a retreat at Eastern Point on the rugged coast of Massachusetts. Another poem, "Quid Pro Quo," would come after meditating on Judas's betrayal of Jesus, my own face taking the place of Judas as I meditated on the Last Supper in John's sublime recounting of the incident.

One keeps coming back to the Scriptures as to a brook, a stream, a river, like the one Ezekiel speaks of as flowing out of the temple precincts toward the east: living water that continually and delightfully refreshes, especially when we are most thirsty. One of the parables I have come back to again and again for refreshment and inspiration is the parable of the prodigal son, recorded in the fifteenth chapter of Luke. It forms the third and most powerful of Jesus' three parables of mercy and comes immediately after the two others: the parable of the lost sheep and the parable of the lost drachma.

"A man had two sons," Jesus begins in Luke's recounting. There is the younger son, rebellious and headstrong, who means to set out on his own with his share of his father's estate. And there is the older, dutiful one, who goes about his father's business working what remains of the estate. It soon becomes evident that the younger son means to have a good time with his half, to seize the day and squander everything. One can look at this story from at least three perspectives: the father's, the younger son's, and the older son's. If you look at it from the father's point of view, you might feel betrayed, sad, disappointed, angry. You might say, OK, you've made your bed, now go lie in it. Or you might feel an incredible sadness at the profound waste of resources and, worse, having to watch your son squander his promise. You would begin to hope each day that your son would come to his senses before it was too late, the way you might worry over an alcoholic or drug-dependent child.

If you are the younger son, you might think, "This is the life," at the same time perhaps wondering what will happen when the money is gone. You might begin learning some hard lessons about fair-weather friends, about being had, about feeling guilty over all you have given up for a pocketful of mirages. You might even begin missing home, your father, even your dutiful older brother who stayed behind to work the farm.

If you are the older son, you might worry about your dumb kid brother, or you might write him off for breaking your father's heart, crippling the estate, and leaving you behind to do the work. You might even begin feeling rather smug and superior for having taken the high road, though if the truth be told all you did was follow your own instinct for survival, which meant earning a living and keeping to the straight and narrow so you didn't wind up in some alley with a knife in your ribs.

In any event, the Las Vegas interlude is over, and the younger son can feel the hard times coming. He is jobless and friendless, and he is in a foreign land with foreign customs. To make matters worse, the real hard times are soon upon him, and the high flyer is now forced to hire himself out to feed pigs. Pigs are unclean animals according to the law, and for Jesus' audience, we have a young Jewish kid lost in the land of the goyim, living a nightmare. Anyone who has ever visited or worked on a farm and seen pigs in their pens and smelled pig slops, knows how far down this kid has spiraled. Recovering alcoholics call it hitting bottom.

Finally, Jesus says, the kid has come to his senses, and a whole world of experience lies in that line alone. And now the kid remembers that even the hired hands on his father's place always had plenty to eat, while here he is, his father's son, dying of hunger. I no longer call you servants, Jesus will tell his disciples at the Last Supper, but heirs. Sons and daughters of my father. Heirs, with a real piece of real estate to come.

Now the kid begins rehearsing what he will do. "Father," he will say, "I have sinned against heaven and against you." He knows he has broken the law and hurt his father. He knows too that he has lost his inheritance and that he is no longer worthy of being called his father's son. But if his father will just treat him as well as he treats the hired hands, he will be satisfied. It is a plan, a last hope, a throwing oneself on the mercy of the very man on whom he has already turned his back.

And as he nears his old home, his father, on the lookout for him, sees his son and is moved to pity. Certainly the father has every right to stand on ceremony, if only to teach his son a lesson. Certainly he might decently wait for the kid to come to him. But the father can see that his son is hurting and so the father— fool that he is—runs to his boy and holds him and kisses him tenderly. Intent on saying what he has been rehearsing these past months, the son manages to get out the first half of his set speech—about no longer deserving to be called his father's son—before the father is ordering his servants to bring out his best robe and sandals and even a ring. He orders the fatted calf killed at once and a feast proclaimed that very day, "because this son of mine was dead and has come back to life; he was lost and is found."

End of story? No. For there is still the other son to consider, the one who stayed home, the one who put in the long hours toiling. He has been out in the fields working, and now, as he approaches the house late in the afternoon, he hears music and dancing from inside. And of course he wants to know who the party is for. Your brother has returned, a servant tells him, and your father has killed the fatted calf because he, your brother, is returned home safe and sound. So what is the older brother's reaction? Relief, happiness, tears? He is angry, and he refuses to join the party or even go in and welcome his brother, so that it is the father who must go out to plead with his older son to welcome his brother back home.

That's right, I have heard some people say out loud or under their breath. Why should he greet the good-for-nothing? The older son has his own self-righteous reply. It is well-reasoned, devastating, hurtful, and seems to have the full weight of the law on his side. "Look," he says, "all these years I have slaved for you" (that is the first exaggeration, for he is a son and not one of the hired hands, but it makes for a good effect) "and never once disobeyed your orders" (which is what in fact he is now doing by refusing to go in to welcome his brother as his father has just pleaded with him to do). "And yet you never offered me so much as a kid for me to celebrate with my friends." Me. Me. Me. And no doubt this is another exaggeration, given the generosity of a father who would turn over half his estate because one of his sons had asked for it. "But for this son of yours—" (not "my poor brother" or even "my brother," but simply, "this son of yours") "—when he comes back after swallowing up your property—he and his women—" (and Jesus has the voice of the self-righteous prig down to perfection) "—you kill the calf we had been fattening."

But fattening for what? For the right celebration? And what better than to celebrate the return of a son, a brother, who was dead and is alive again? And the father? Does he call on the weight of the law that demands that children honor their parents? Or the law which says that a wastrel son who will not listen to his parents might be taken out and stoned by the community, as Deuteronomy insists? And so the father pleads with his older a second time. "My son," he says, "you are with me always and all I have is yours." And yet, as he appeals to his son in the name of justice, it is a justice indistinguishable from what is at the heart of justice: mercy. "It was only right," he says, "that we should celebrate and rejoice, because your brother here was dead and has come to life, he was lost and is found."

What happened then? Did the son relent and go in? Did he welcome his brother warmly or merely curl his lip and extend a cold formal handshake? Or did he finally realize the miracle of what had happened: that his brother had had a profound change of heart and was ready now to begin again, simply as a hired hand, and all the wiser for his mistakes? Or did the older son go in, but take a "Let's wait and see" approach, wondering if the kid would revert to his old ways once he had been fed and taken back, like some dry drunk who you know is going to go on another bender?

And the younger son. How does he feel? Does he know that he will have to work hard even to begin to regain his brother's trust, to say nothing of his love? How long, if ever, will it be before he can actually forgive himself? And what of the father, who loves his sons and dotes on them and broods on them as a mother hen on her young? Will he ever stop caring for either of them, even if they should go on hurting him as in fact both have? What an extraordinary picture of a father, unheard of in the ancient world. The Gospel settles on none of these scenarios, which is part of its beauty and the force of how it works on us.

And where do we situate ourselves in all this? Do we, having hurt and disappointed others, identify more with the younger son? Have we ever had to ask forgiveness for our betrayal of others, including those closest to us? Or are we more like the older son, doing what has been enjoined upon us to do, dutiful, following the law, paying tithes and taxes, working, but always keeping tabs, so that, if we are asked to welcome back our fallen brother, we can say to our father, "Well, you never once so much as . . . "? Or as we grow older and have children of our own, do we identify more with the father, who almost cannot believe his good fortune that his son has returned alive and is the wiser for his experience, so that we have a party at once to celebrate the good news?

Over the years the story has taken on different configurations for me. At different times I have found myself identifying with each of the characters in turn. There were times when my heart was lifted by the story to make amends, and times when I identified with the small, tight-lipped, uncharitable claims of the older son. There are even times when I have celebrated the loveliness and foolishness of a Father who so cares for us that he forgives us as soon as we ask for that forgiveness, no matter how low we have sunk.

But the Gospel story does not stop resonating there either. After all, there is also the teller of the tale to consider, and it is Jesus himself who in Luke's recounting tells this story about his Father. So where does Jesus fit into this story about fathers and sons? I suppose he is in some ways closer to the dutiful son, at least in obeying the Father and doing his will day in and day out. But we would hardly mistake the one good son for the other. When I compare the selflessness and radical self-effacement of the Son of Man with the posture taken by the older son, I am brought near to tears. For here is a son, we know, who would go in and celebrate the return of his brother.

In fact, there would be no reproachful son, for son and father would be at one in rejoicing over the return of the younger brother, who was dead and has come back to life. More, Jesus is a brother—a prodigal lover—who left everything to go in search of his lost brothers and sisters. Is this then not an insight into the unity of Father, Son, and Holy Spirit? Was it not the Spirit that moved the son to get up out of the pigpen and begin all over again, and the Father who rejoiced to see his boy again and went out and led him into the banquet? Does not this Son stand in for all of us and rejoice over the lost sheep, lost coin, lost child?

But the story does not end there either. The metaphorical phrasing, "your brother here was dead and has come to life," must also resonate for us. It may be Jesus' admonishment to his Jewish brothers to embrace the lost tribes—Samaritans, yes, but also Syrians and Egyptians and Philistines (for which read Palestinians), as well as Greeks and Cypriots and Romans and Macedonians. And more: One might be dead but be brought back to life again, like the very teller of this tale, who, though never a criminal or miscreant, would shortly be handled like one and given a criminal's death.

A stone, then. A cornerstone, hitting the water, and sending ripple after ripple outward to touch us in successive waves. It is a story so simple that anyone hearing it—and it has been heard and reflected upon now by billions of listeners—would understand it and its challenges at once. It is a story so profound that it keeps on resonating no matter how many times we read it or have heard it from the pulpit. And yet it is only one of thousands of such passages that the Bible holds, ready to work their wonder on us. This reminds me of how the monks would come to their fathers—their Abbas—and beg for a word from the Scriptures before returning to their cells to meditate on it. No, not meditate only, but live with the word until the Word—God's flame—ignited in them. In time, if they were fortunate enough, they would stand cleansed and purified until at last they could feel their hearts burning within their chests, and they would look again in astonished joy to see themselves turning into living flame.

LARRY WOIWODE

GOD'S IMMANENCE
IN CREATION

WHEN I WAS TWELVE and what happens to boys had not happened to me yet, I loved to walk alone. I would walk five miles down a railroad track to my grandparents' place or walk seven miles in the opposite direction to a lake I liked to look at, after I had walked to the four corners of our town a half dozen times that day. It was not beyond me to walk twenty miles a day without even stopping to think about it, as I have not, really, until now.

The places I liked to walk most were outside the sign of any habitation, in the carved gap of a railroad line or along a dirt road that led through pastures and fields to a woods. When I walked I liked to think about others who had walked before me and about the only ones I had heard of who had walked as much as I did. These were the apostles who followed Jesus Christ, along with Jesus, of course, and a United States President who

once lived not far from the area in Illinois where my family settled, Abraham Lincoln.

The place I loved above all to walk was a woods halfway
between my grandparents' home and the lake I liked, straight
north of those two points, or so it seemed to me then, though I
believe its actual direction was west. I walked toward it along the
edge of a road that was such pure sand it was as hard to walk on
as if it had been dunes or the sand of an unpacked beach. All
along the route, hedge apples lay in the sand like limes so bloat-
ed that the pebbling of their peels looked like worms locked in
swollen swirls. They struck the sand like shot puts, and if you
kicked one it was about as heavy, and it left a sap of sticky goo on
your shoe or bare toes. Hedgerows crowded the road along the
perimeter of the State Forest for which I was headed; they grew
wild in this place that seemed to me like the Sahara, deserted.

Once I had sized up my route for the next mile or so, or to the
next hill or curve, I never looked ahead of my feet as I walked. I
don't know why. What flowed past or flew in from the side or
swung up to encounter me was more of a surprise that way, I
guess. I partly wanted to be surprised, or safely scared, as most
boys that age do—a natural scare that never approached a terror
I lived with. My mother was dead and had died away from home
of an illness or disease I had never been able to fathom and my
father had never been able to explain, so it was as if my worst
thoughts about her had sent her off and caused her death.

The latticework of shadow from the hedge-apple rows thick-
ened to trunks and overarching shadows of trees, tall elms still
safe from disease, maples, burr oaks going gnarled, horse chest-
nuts, and a dozen other varieties our science teacher pointed out
on a field trip when I was so overtaken by the trees themselves I
could not take in their names.

But I knew them as well as aunts and uncles, or so I felt then, as I took more and more walks through the State Forest that was also becoming a wildlife sanctuary. I felt so much at home I would sing as I sang nowhere else, sometimes mere notes that hoped to reach the tones and patterns of plainsong—this I loved, mixed with incense, as much as anything about the church.

"Oh, beautiful trees!" I sang. "Oh, sky above me! Oh, earth beneath my feet." It was really a shout, tones or blasts of true assurance. I sang the same song each time I walked here, as if to announce my presence to the elements I addressed—the sky and earth, the two that seemed to govern my life from its beginning.

I was never afraid and never lost my way, no matter how many and how varied the routes I took, and I never felt the sense of loss or absence of my mother that I did everywhere else. She was from the plains, far from any woods, where an individual tree was rare and offered shade, but too many got in your way and were a bother or threat. I grew up and walked with her in the spaces of the plains and at the edges of woods, the blue-green cascades of Minnesota mostly, and the movement and placement of her limbs as she walked seemed to communicate some of her feelings about plains and woods. But people, I learned, were made to talk, unlike the spaces of earth, both those empty and those filled-up. These seemed to want so much to talk they caused me to listen as I did not with people, not even her.

Now as I walked and sang, matching the words to the pace of my walk, I saw rough trunks crowd close, their shadows lying on leaves and needles they had shed, all of this intertwining in a way that gave the light that I saw striking my feet more substance. The chill of a presence slid over me as if I were shedding leaves myself, and I stopped and looked up, in the presence of God, and watched the trees in their breadth and height mounting even closer to him. All the patterns of the scribbled multitude of branching twigs and the matching gaps of designated light that arranged themselves around or in relationship to the other were as much a song or shout of praise as the simple song I shouted. This was the earth, these the trees in a multitude of beauty, the sky and the space so brimming with angels and voices, it seemed, they would break into appearance or speech at any moment. I experienced no terror, but a sense of being gripped by something of greater substance than my mother's arms, and sometimes tears of laughter would leap out like the presences I expected to appear.

One presence was here, I saw, as I turned with my face raised, in these trees and the sky, in the earth that supported me. All this had been put in place for my pleasure, and so that the God I loved could teach me about myself and him. I had been taught to love him, but the words of the language that I knew were English, and they could not approach the language that poured from everything around with a familiarity that aroused in me a word-less love. It was a love that for the life of me I could not define but was given a glimpse of when I later read, *The Heavens declare the glory of God. . . . Day unto day utters speech. . . . There is no speech or language where their voice is not heard. . . . For since the creation of the world his invisible attributes are clearly seen, being understood by the things that are made. . . . For by him all things were created that are in heaven and that are on earth, visible and invisible, whether thrones or principalities or powers. All things were created through him and for him. And he is before all things, and in him all things consist.*

Here were two languages put partially into English. What they communicated in the language I partly knew is so unimaginable—especially that last statement—that I am jolted from that earlier time and left flat-footed in the present.

That last statement has been so seldom touched upon by any portion of Christendom you would think it does not exist, and you may look it over and turn it every way you wish but it will still say "in him all things consist." How am I able to reconcile this with my now pragmatic and fainthearted, tone-deaf view of nature—my hard-heartedness toward grass and trees and birds and fish and beasts and bracken and oceans and rivers of ice and stormy winds fulfilling his word? Lopped off from that boy who had not learned to reason and did not yet pay more attention to his own body and its developments than to the developed creation around him, I seem farther from the truth of what those passages state than do those who worshiped trees or imaginary or real spirits trapped inside them.

Those who practiced worship of that kind missed the central truth that most of the above passages also teach: There is much more than trees or the real or imaginary spirits trapped in them, when you understand they are manifestations or communications of the actual Christ.

Carefully and with the greatest accuracy you can, write a description of your favorite six-foot patch of creation or nature or, if your spirit is feeling expansive, favorite ten square acres. If anyone who reads it after you are done does not sense in your description some of the hidden attributes of God, which we are told exist and which all of us know exist but try to deny because they do not fit with the fullness of rationalism that enlightened thinking (rather than the language of God) has brought to us, then our description is a failure in the face of God. Language was given to us so that we can return to God the language his creation is proclaiming to us—we who can hear only when we are surrounded by upscale stereo equipment.

On some days, if I lie for hours on the earth or crawl on my belly through tall grass or weeds or walk into a forest where I might get lost and lie down and take a nap and then wake—on some of those days I sense again those voices that communicated to me from all sides when I went walking in the woods as a boy. Did you—Do you ever roll in new-mown grass and feel the reek of its greenness fill your nostrils so much it seems your nose will bleed, and then you realize the reeking is the blood of grass, or something even more astonishing that your grip on language has not yet been able to grasp?

There are times when, with a warning in my legs of a spongy weakness, the earth beneath me is revealed as molecular, able to give way at any second, when every gesture and word formed and even every thought is being weighed and measured (right foot, left foot) on shifting scales that are accurate to infinity. How can I escape now? The giving earth itself is God's handiwork, and our treading on it is communicated through a network so precise that even our mightiest computers cannot begin to calculate it. We sense this and tend to rest on its evidence even when it remains unseen.

This is faith.

In whom do I have faith?

I have faith in God.

Where is God?

God is everywhere.

Then why don't I bump into him or step on him?

You do, in a sense, but you would not know it, most likely, if he himself appeared in front of you.

God is everywhere as the Spirit he is. This is the age of the Spirit he has given the world through and by and for his Son. Even though the world came into being for God's purpose, the world does not know him or recognize him or receive him or the message the handiwork of his world continues to give in every detail we are able to see.

A glimpse of this message was given to a poet who had suffered the rigors of the Soviet Gulag and was trying to read an anthology of modern English poetry despite his faulty command of the language. He says, "I remember sitting there in the small wooden shack, peering through the square, porthole-size window at the wet, muddy, dirt road with a few stray chickens on it, half believing what I'd just read, half wondering whether my grasp of English wasn't playing tricks on me. I had there a veritable boulder of an English-Russian dictionary, and I went through its pages time and again, checking every word, every allusion, hoping that they might spare me the meaning that stared at me from the page. I guess I was simply refusing to believe that way back in 1939 an English poet had said, 'Time . . . worships language,' and yet the world around was still what it was."

The speaker is Joseph Brodsky, the Nobel laureate. He wants to make clear the effect on him of that distilled statement from W.H. Auden's "In Memory of W.B. Yeats": "time worships language." Brodsky abhorred artifice and sham and was so attuned to language, especially the language of Scripture, that he saw the statement as so revolutionary it should have altered the known world. Time is the lesser compatriot to language and so time, whom many personify and revere as a god, bows to language, is helpless before language, because language is older and greater and with it people build adornments that last and will last while time merely passes away—just as God through language, the breath of his Word, formed worlds that endure and will last through eternity. A Russian poet grasped this on first sight under straitened conditions while it flies past most of us—with the thrumming beat and glide at least of a flicker, I hope, like the bird with its yellow-gold ribs and that flash of red you cannnot miss.

When I remember how I drew in as if in gulps the words of Brodsky as he explained his struggle toward what was a transformation, I can see my feet moving through the woods and hear the words of the song that was given to me. Just as Brodsky, in arriving by the labored steps of strange words to the understanding that transformed him, could not believe the world had remained the same, so when I wrote "I feel a pressure behind and turn and there are the cottonwoods and willows at the far end of the street, along the edge of the lake, flying the maidenhair faces of their leaves into the wind, and beyond their crowns of trembling insubstantiality, across the lake dotted with cottonwood pollen, the blue and azure plain abuts against the horizon at infinity"—when I wrote this and then read it, I knew I would never be the same. It was a time when the balancing scales beneath were jiggling so much I was sure they would give way as Christ in God was revealed to me. Then began the search for a way to rest in him.

But we forget and become deadened, as I have said. Or I do, and I even walk around whispering, sure, God's everywhere, that's why my life's so wonderful—not said in faith but in a detached and abstract cynicism so bitter it can burn holes in the air. It was when I had reached a moment like that, once again, a year ago, that my wife said, "Will you pray, please?" Sure, I thought, sure, I'll pray, and lit into a prayer with such anger a hole indeed seemed to open to the presence I had forgotten, no, abandoned, and suddenly I felt more than the ladder of Jacob with angels ascending and descending on it. The pure power of Christ's spirit poured down on me with such force that prayers for my wife and children, who had gathered, were pressed from me as prayer had never been squeezed from me, as it felt, in fifty years. When I was finished and looked up, it was as if I were seeing each of my family for the first time, transformed.

They were clearly his, as I was, or his much more than I. They had waited for this confirmation, I saw, and I had been too cautious and rational and justifiably bitter (if I could have explained my state in words) to give in to power mightier than time, the Word.

I went to bed. It was all that I could do. But in bed I could not sleep. Then the pressure that had once caused me to turn in recognition exerted only a bit of its real weight, as I sensed, and I could not move. I lay under the pressure, now like a molecular current containing yet revivifying me, and every petty sin looked like an electron above an abyss in the magnificence of the current that kept flowing down and through me. I could not move for hours. Everyone I had sinned against or hated or could not forgive appeared over the night, not visibly, not so I could see them, but I sensed the presencë of each and knew who it was and was astonished and grieved at the smallness of my sin in the weighty glory of the forgiveness I had received and was receiving. Tears ran from my staring eyes in silence and soaked the bed, but I was locked in such joy I felt if this is the end, so be it. It was the end in one way, perhaps (you will find me as unforgiving and petty as always, I suspect, the next time we meet), because I understood I was being called to walk.

I could not move but I had to. Once I was out of bed—and barely made it from the room (never waking my wife; she never woke this whole night)—I slowly walked the perimeter of two small rooms and a hall, my pacing grounds, and was given a partial sense of bearing in a body the weight of glory for a few steps, all I could bear. I realized I had been prepared for this by that turn, that sense of pressure, but more so I now recognize by those walks in the woods where I watched my feet lit by light from the sun as I listened to the language of creation leaping past time and entering me in a beginning I could not explain until now.

CROSSINGS

LUCI
SHAW

LIVING IN THE GAP
EXPLORING THE SPACE BETWEEN
EARTH AND HEAVEN

MY FATHER, A PREACHER by both calling and disposition, would often deliver this axiomatic advice to whoever happened to be listening—"Beware of being so heavenly-minded that you're no earthly use." I've never quite fallen into that trap; my inclinations tend to favor earthly-mindedness. Nevertheless both history and theology provide evidence of a discontinuity between the two states (of mind and/or spirit or reality), a lacuna which seems to demand exploration. If we are to stand within the framework of Christian belief we are required to take both earth and heaven seriously, and, moreover, to attempt to find connections that bridge the gap between the two.

Learning to be amphibious, that is, adapting to life in two radically divergent realms, heavenly and earthly, demands of us that we learn to see again, through different lenses than those to which we have become accustomed. As a member of our egregiously human species, with all the limitations that apply, I must, if I lay claim to life eternal, acquire vision, see beyond the physical boundaries, get ready to be translated.

Enoch and Moses—unlike Adam, unlike most of us—moved seamlessly from restricted terrestrial living into the presence of freedom and life in its optimum dimension in the presence of God.

Yet here *we* are, day by day attempting the utterly impossible. We are called to perform the rash absurdities of the redeemed, or perish miserably. In effect Christ calls us to "perform impossibilities or perish," like the fig tree that came under the curse of his displeasure. We are responsible somehow to demonstrate that it is possible to bring heaven to earth by living the life of grace in an ungraceful place, by gluing together the seen and the unseen. We are required to be links with the unlinkable, with otherwise disparate entities. As Arthur Koestler says, in *The Sleepwalkers*, "It is a perverse mistake to identify the religious need solely with intuition and emotion, science solely with the logical and rational. Prophets and discoverers, painters and poets all share this amphibial quality of living both in the contoured drylands and in the boundless ocean."[1]

I wrote a poem about this double identity, once. Identifying myself with an amphibian, a frog which can survive in neither water nor air for more than minutes at a time, I laid claim to that Scripture verse which tells me that in my mortal state I have "no continuing city" (Hebrews 13:14).

The Amphibian

Warm
after a while on a rock,
drunk with sky, her green silk
shrivels with wind. With a wet,

singular sound, then, she creases
the silver film, turns fluid,
her webbed toes accomplishing
the dark dive to water bottom and
the long soak, until her lungs,
spun for air, urge her up
for breath.

She moves
in two worlds, caught between
upper and under, never home.
Restless: skin withering for wet,
and the nether ooze,
or nostrils aching to fill
with free air her bubble lungs,
heart thumping, tympanum
throat pulsing to flood
the darkening sky with loud
frog song.[2]

Some of us have experienced this. There have been moments when, like Paul carried into the third heaven, we have been off guard enough to be swept from our pedestrian stance, to have grown wings, or to be quite suddenly able to walk on water, blood surging, the light we move into so different from ordinary daylight, so bright around us that we are burned, aware that grace has seized us and carried us away (I am reminded of my high school Latin definition of *rapio*—to seize and carry off) to a state in which everything is changed. It is a foretaste of the Second Coming. Jesus is here. Jesus has lifted us into a new dimension.

But the moment ebbs away. The epiphany is snuffed out. Once again we are on an earth imperturbably solid and unyield-

173

ing, and we are back to groping in shadow again and seeing only through a glass, darkly.

Perhaps this is because we are not yet ready for unfiltered light. Think how difficult and even dangerous it is to look the sun in the eye; we have to squint through smoked glass even to attempt it. And it is an infinitely more fearful thing to approach God face to face. Moses, though a friend of Yahweh, had to be sheltered in a crack in the shoulder of the mountain, with the hand of the Almighty shielding him from the glory blaze, learning firsthand what it means to say that "no one can see God at any time" and live. Others who frontally encountered heavenly reality found themselves wanting. Daniel fell to the ground paralyzed with fear in the presence of Yahweh's messenger. Saint John, on Patmos, opens his account of an astonishing supernatural revelation by quoting the instructions from the "one like the Son of Man" who told him "Fear not, write what you see," and afterward, again, "Fear not, write what you have seen." Nearly all the angels in the early chapters of Luke's Gospel preface their appearances or their messages with the reassurance, "Fear not," as did our Lord himself as he walked toward his friends in the boat on wild Galilee, asking them to watch him rather than the engulfing waves. In each case the fear was warranted. The fear was as real as the vision.

To be a seer or a prophet is to be called to a double identity, almost a split personality. As he looks upward the seer receives a vision. Then, as prophet, he must shift his gaze to earth and proclaim the oracle to the waiting but often recalcitrant populace. The poet Christian, the visionary writer, must stand with the seer and the prophet, one foot in heaven, one on earth, likewise centered on both spheres at once, perpetually torn by this dual focus as divine dreams are channeled through eyes and ears to pen or vocal chords. I bear witness to the reality of the prophet's burden; consciously or not most of my writing springs in obedience to the mandate, "Fear not, write what you see."

But God is Spirit. How, with our limited senses, may we see such an ephemeral entity? And why, if God wants us to trust him, to know him, does he seem deliberately to conceal or disguise himself? Why is truth often presented as "mystery"? The prophet Isaiah cries out in seeming frustration, "Verily, thou art a God that hidest thyself" (Isa. 45:15), and the writer of the Proverbs proclaims a paradox—"It is the glory of God to conceal a matter" (Prov. 25:2). If we had been God we would not have done it like that, we tell ourselves. People perish where the vision has been dimmed or extinguished. It would seem vital to the divine-human relationship to preserve the flow of ideas and images from above if human beings are to retain a sense of the divine image in themselves and to be capable of dialogue with the Creator.

Yet the messages kept coming, channeled through exceptional individuals whose role as spokespersons for the Almighty was never a comfortable one. Prophetic Biblical passages are almost invariably couched in words like these: "The *vision* of Isaiah," "the *word* of the LORD, which Isaiah *saw*," "the Lord GOD *showed* Amos, and behold . . . ," "an *oracle* . . . the *vision* of Nahum," "the *burden* of God which Habakkuk *saw*." Daniel saw "visions in his head as he lay on his bed" and he was told to "write the dream down." We are not surprised to learn from Hebrews 1 that "in many and various ways God spoke to our fathers by the prophets." But the oracle, the heavenly message, was commonly mediated to the Biblical writer by means of words or visions—what he heard or what he saw, or both.

The question arises: Why was an intermediary, such as a prophet, necessary for the message to be transmitted? Why was the Word not spoken or seen directly, in its full blaze of light and sound and color and meaning, to the entire community? Certain reasons suggest themselves.

First, there is the difficulty already mentioned of a fragile, vulnerable human being facing the God of glory. As Emily Dickinson succinctly phrased it: "The Truth must dazzle gradually / or every man be blind—" and in C.S. Lewis's words: "God is the only comfort; he is also the supreme terror: the thing we most need and the thing we most want to hide from. He is our only ally and we have made ourselves his enemies. Some people talk as if meeting the gaze of Absolute Goodness would be fun. They need to think again."[3] My good friend Walter Hearn remembers a conversation with a Baptist colleague who had become a high-church Anglican. Hearn remarked to his friend that he found all the liturgical apparatus distracting, that it got in the way of his direct experience of God. "Of course it does, you ninny!" his friend replied. "That's what it's there for. God is too glorious to be apprehended directly. The liturgy, the robes, the incense, the chanting are to enable you to stand in the presence of God without being bowled over by the power." A full, frontal view of the Almighty, swift as light, sharp and intense as a laser, with the energy of the universe flashing from his eyes, and with the Earth, and us on it, cradled like a marble in his palm, would paralyze, flatten, and annihilate us.

Yet here we are, hale and whole, and every day God shows us his goodness, just as he promised Moses ("I will make my goodness pass before you"). It is visible not only in the Biblical images he projects of himself (shepherd, mother hen, protective fortress, banner, evergreen tree) but in the very fact that *they are pictures*. With Virginia Stem Owens we ask, "Give me phenomena. . . . Give me pictures and models. . . . The one thing I cannot take is the denying darkness and the blind man's eye."

And here the benison of the sacramental view of life is evident. As we read in the *Imitation of Christ*, "If your heart is straight with God, then every creature will be to you a mirror of life and a book of holy doctrine." The created universe is crammed with pointers, clues to the nature and creator-ship of this invisible Maker. Even in the way the Scriptures are written—one-third of it in poetry, vivid storytelling in the parables, and even the most rigorous apostolic teaching illuminated by metaphor, analogy, illustration—we receive an indication of the goodness of God in the vivid ways he informs the human imagination, that faculty of ours that sees pictures in our heads almost like colored slides projected on a screen. God, who knows us better than we know ourselves, is not content to speak simply to the rational intelligence, but informs us through imagination and intuition. Where doctrinal principles seem logical, though abstract, images print themselves on our minds and even on our senses in such brilliant color and three-dimensional texture that time and distraction cannot obliterate them. The parables of Jesus are not meant to be dissected analytically; they are designed to be taken in through the senses and the imagination—the windows of the soul—and *felt*, their subtext of ideal, principle, and theological truth absorbed almost unconsciously as the mental image suffuses the understanding over a period of time, a kind of divine soft-sell salesmanship.

But while figurative language often leaves us with vivid impressions and clarifies abstractions by giving us a picture, or telling us a story, or teaching effectively by analogy, it may also obscure what is being said. The truth is often hidden behind the screen of metaphor. God does not always speak openly, plainly, simply, directly, as he did through Noah and Moses and Jonah. The prophetic writings are replete with enigmatic or oblique messages. One sometimes wonders why the divine directives were transmitted at all if they were so cryptic. The prophecies of Ezekiel and the Revelation of Saint John in particular often seem like hallucinatory ravings. Why lampstands and burning swords? Why the tantalizing riddles about vials and scrolls and bowls and seals and pale horses and scarlet women and lightnings and crystal seas in the Revelation, if it is supposed to *reveal* something? Why the bizarre "wheels within wheels full of eyes" of Ezekiel? Why all those unearthly beasts with their hybrid wings and horns and hooves and talons?

Jesus gives us one clue why. The Gospel of Mark records that "with many parables he spoke the word [to the people]. . . . He did not speak to them without a parable, but privately to his own disciples he explained everything" (Mark 4:34). In Matthew's Gospel Jesus' followers asked him, "Why do you speak to them in parables?" Jesus' answer: "To you it has been given to know the secrets of the kingdom of heaven, but to them it has not been given. . . . This is why I speak to them in parables, because seeing they do not see, and hearing they do not hear, nor do they understand. With them is fulfilled the prophecy of Isaiah which says: You shall indeed hear but never understand, and you shall indeed see but never perceive. For this people's heart has grown dull and their ears heavy of hearing, and their eyes they have closed. . . . But blessed are your eyes, for they see, and your ears, for they hear" (Matt. 13:10-16). Jesus made a clear distinction between those who want to hear and understand, who yearn to see and believe, and those who deliberately clap their hands over their ears or shut out any illumination with tightly closed eyes. The sense organs, which have been created to receive revelation, may become atrophied through disuse, and the result is indifference and dullness to the colorful inner landscape of creative insight.

However, it is not always a matter of our choice to see or not to see, to hear or not to hear. It almost seems as if God is capricious, showing himself openly from time to time (and of course, most purposefully and powerfully of all in the Incarnation), and hiding himself, "dwelling in darkness," at other times in what seems to our human perception an arbitrary way. I wrote this poem in Christchurch Cathedral in Oxford, in the small, decrepit chapel of an eighth-century woman who was the patron saint of Oxford. Every other part of the cathedral had been beautifully restored, but the poem tells the story of age and neglect, and of my own longing to make sense of the fragmentary ceiling fresco:

St Frideswide's Chapel

In this ancient place
one section of the fresco
ceiling has been left
to peel, a puzzle, half
the pieces lost. As from
the bottom of a well I stare
up, waiting for revelation.
A raw plaster frowns
from the past, a closed sky, murky
as thunder, traced with

gold shreds—a snatch
of hair, a broken chin line,
wing fragments in red, in blue.
My eyes are busy—deepening
pigment, filling in the detail
of hands, feathers, touching up
the face of an angel. But nothing
changes. The terrible inscrutability
endures, deeper than
groined arches. Tattered

seraphim flash their diminishing
edges, like the chiaroscuro God who,
if we believe Michelangelo, touched
Adam into being with one finger,
whose footprints crease the blackness
of Genesaret, whose wing feathers
brush our vaulted heaven, purple
with storm, whose moon
is smudged—a round, glass window,
an eye moving between clouds.[4]

The God who is not there. Or, the God who is *there* but not *here,* except for occasional momentary visitations. I have often felt, in reflective moments as well as at the raw edge of experience, that I have a now-you-see-him, now-you-don't God, a chiaroscuro God. Some of his features are highlighted, in the manner of the Italian Renaissance painters who employed that technique, but his being exhibits such mystery, such inscrutability, such otherness, that it can be represented only by deep shadow, which might as well signal absence as obscurity it is so unknowable. The word *chiaroscuro* is itself an oxymoron—*chiaro* (clear, or light) combined with *oscuro* (dark). It suggests ambiguity and paradox, a fitting term for a deity who has revealed himself in the flesh yet walks in mystery, who scatters clues and hints to his being throughout Creation, Holy Scripture, and the human mind, leaving his burning footprints on the lake, but then withdrawing.

And we are supposed to *trust our lives* to this enigma? That is all very well for the author of *The Cloud of Unknowing,* but what of those of us who are pragmatic realists rather than mystics? And am I the only one who feels puzzled and in jeopardy because of this conundrum?

We yearn for union with God, for the sense of safety and

belonging that should be a given in the Father-child relationship. What we often experience instead is frustration and aloneness. Psychiatrist Gerald May speaks to this tension: "We have
this idea that everyone should be totally independent, totally
whole, totally together spiritually, and totally fulfilled. That is a
myth. In reality, our lack of fulfillment is the most precious gift
we have. It is the source of our passion, our creativity, our search
for God. All the best of life comes out of *our human yearning—
our not being satisfied.* Certainly Scripture and religious tradition point out that we are not to be satisfied. We are meant to go
on looking and seeking."[5]

Oh, yes! I find myself saying. That is it exactly. It is the *longing* to know who God is, to know *him*, to look him in the eye as
friend with friend, to be in conversation with him, that draws us
like a magnet. The idea of the Promised Land kept the Hebrew
people going for forty years in the wilderness. If they had known
nothing but satisfaction, and contentment, and answered prayer,
and fig trees, and vineyards, and milk and honey, what would
have motivated them to keep going? If all I know is sunlight
without shadow, will I fail to appreciate it? Might I even feel
bored with the monotony of continuous light?

Gerald May's ideas bring me some comfort. But I would go
even further than he. In studying the Beatitude which describes
the blessing of being hungry and thirsty for righteousness, I have
wondered if that hunger and thirst had something to do with the
longing C.S. Lewis talks about: *sehnsucht,* the desire to experience some poignant, holy, intangible beauty that is indescribable
but for the conviction that when we find it the joy will make
sense of all the heartache and darkness and emptiness of our
present existence.

Sometimes, and again I speak from personal experience, the
feeding of our hunger, the slaking of our thirst feels agonizingly

slow. There are seasons when God seems to impart himself to me, as in the Eucharist—crumb by crumb, sip by sip, allowing me just enough of himself, just enough nourishment to keep me alive. Sometimes I am Hansel or Gretel following the sparse trail of crumbs to find home.

No Backtrack, Hansel

Truth is a wilderness where your skills
and your dry wit seem not enough
to find a path on pathless hills.
Behind you leave such tenuous stuff—
such a sparse trail of shining stones
shown by time's black birds to be bread
for scavengers. And no blank bones
mark where your unfleshed dreams lie dead.
Emptiness is the harsh rebuff
and doubt the wilderness where your will
and withered wit seem not enough
to find paths on this pathless hill.[7]

Ron Hansen, in *Mariette in Ecstasy*, suggests "how important it is for God to be away from us and be the one we pine for but cannot have, for *desiring God invigorates us*. Desiring him but never fully having him we cannot grow tired or slack. We know the joy of his 'hereness' now and then, but were his distance and indifference all we had, it would still be sufficient if we sought and cherished it."[7] Blaise Pascal tells us that "a religion which does not affirm that God is hidden is not true." *Vere tu es Deus absconditus.* Even the Annunciation, that announcement of the arrival of Light into the world, had its shadow side. In Greek the language is plain. The Angel spoke prophetically to Mary, telling her, "The power of the Most High will *overshadow* you" (Luke 1:35).

The Overshadow

When we think of God, and
angels, and the Angel
we suppose ineffable light.

So there is surprise in the air
when we see him bring to Mary,
in her lit room, a gift of darkness.

What is happening under that
huge wing of shade? In that mystery
what in-breaking wildness fills her?

She is astonished and afraid; even in
that secret twilight she bends her head,
hiding her face behind the curtain

of her hair; she knows that
the rest of her life will mirror
this blaze, this sudden midnight.[8]

Cleopas and his friend, on the way to Emmaus, were per-
plexed about Jesus' fate and disappearance—Jesus, who had
been their hope for Israel and her liberation, was no longer with
them. The hope had vanished. Then Jesus showed up and
walked with them, even breaking bread with them, but at the
moment when "their eyes were opened and they recognized
him" he disappeared from their sight. As soon as they understood, he was gone! God's greatest acts may leave us hanging.
We, like those friends of Jesus, have glimpses of knowing, of seeing something transcendent that confirms our faith. But because
it is *faith*—which has to do with things not yet seen—we also
must live with the Biblical experience of being left in the lurch.

Is this all by divine design? Can I affirm, with C.S. Lewis, that "my best havings are wantings"? In *The Problem of Pain*, Lewis comes even closer to this feeling of being magnetized by heaven and its promises: "There have been times when I think we do not desire heaven; but more often I find myself wondering whether, in our heart of hearts, we have ever desired anything else. . . . It is the secret signature of each soul, the incommunicable and unappeasable want, the thing we desired before we met our wives or made our friends or chose our work, and which we shall still desire on our deathbeds."[9]

So. We live, still amphibious, but in a place of faith and prophetic hope. The darkness, the hunger, the thirst, the desire—all make a void, a vacuum by which our hearts are inevitably drawn toward the fulfillment of that want. We glimpse the transcendent momentarily. It is an appetizer; we are teased into wanting more; in the temporal hiatus between fierce desire and realization we live in hope until we are sprung from the trap like birds released from a cage into the limitless sky, until the end of the matter, whose eternal timing only God knows.

NOTES

[1] Arthur Koestler, *The Sleepwalkers: A History of Man's Changing Vision of the Universe* (New York: Viking Penguin, 1990), n.p.

[2] Luci Shaw, *Polishing the Petoskey Stone* (Wheaton, IL: Harold Shaw, 1990), 3.

[3] C.S. Lewis, *Mere Christianity* 1:5 (New York: MacMillan, 1952), 24.

[4] Luci Shaw, *Writing the River* (Colorado Springs: Pinon Press, 1994), 21.

[5] Gerald G. May, interview in *The Wittenberg Door*, Sept/Oct 1992, 7-10.

[6] Shaw, *Polishing the Petoskey Stone*, 64.

[7] Ron Hansen, *Mariette in Ecstasy* (New York: HarperCollins, 1991), 60-61.

[8] Shaw, *Writing the River*, 23.

[9] C.S. Lewis, *The Problem of Pain* (London: Geoffrey Bles, 1944), 133.

DORIS
BETTS

MEMENTO MORI

MURIEL SPARK'S THIRD NOVEL, the macabre but sharply witty
Memento Mori (1959),[1] has three epigraphs; the first two by
Yeats and Traherne are about old age, while the third from *The
Penny Catechism* is as follows:

Q. What are the four last things to be ever remembered?
A. The four last things to be ever remembered are
   Death, Judgement, Hell, and Heaven.

Spark, who was thirty-nine before she published any fiction,
had converted to Roman Catholicism five years before, calling
the Church "something to measure from" rather than a direct
source of inspiration. But the "four last things" are not listed as
such in Scripture, as eschatology had been developed by that

very Church out of Jesus' references to apocalypse (largely in Matthew 24–25), bits of Isaiah and Daniel, and especially the Book of Revelation.

Spark might well have added an epigraph from the psychology of C.G. Jung, for in this novel all her characters are not merely old, but some are senile; and Jung held the view that anyone in old age who did not focus on the goal of death was probably neurotic. By Jung's definition, most of Spark's characters are.

The aging old friends and rivals live in the quarrelsome past, prolong old literary arguments and jealousies, jockey to inherit wealth, snipe at society and one another, employ silly substitutes for former sexual vitality, collect encyclopedic but insignificant research on the process of aging, and when blackmailed either keep or reveal secrets the reader judges to be trivial. In short, these elders meditate on everything except their own imminent deaths.

Besides this cluster of superficial friends and kin in the 75 to 85 age bracket, twelve old ladies (called by nurses "the Grannies") survive but wet their beds in the government-subsidized Maud Long Medical Ward. The dozen includes Miss Jean Taylor, formerly a maid-companion and acquaintance of that larger senior group still able to live independently outside old-age institutions. Both Taylor and retired Chief Inspector Henry Mortimer receive the whispered fears of the rest as, one by one, they begin receiving phone messages from an anonymous caller who says only, "Remember you must die!" and then hangs up. To every person the caller reveals a different tone, accent, apparent age or class.

After Dame Lettie Colson is bludgeoned to death during a random robbery, police try to link these spreading telephone calls to some actual stalker preying on the elderly, but wiretaps and detective work fail. Both Mortimer and Taylor decide the strange caller must be Death himself, or else a personification rising from the subconscious of each victim on whom death is persistently laying claim, despite their denials of mortality. During his own conscientious investigation, policeman Mortimer remarks that if he had his life to live over he would "compose himself every night by practicing the remembrance of death," because that practice intensifies life. "Without it," he adds, "you might as well live on the whites of eggs."

And when one visitor to the old ladies' home, who is also plagued by the unknown caller, suggests that Jean Taylor's quick mind with its history of sophistication must hate to be remanded by arthritis to this collection of drooling, incoherent wards of the state, she calls those other eleven grannies her own "memento mori—like your phone calls."

Supernatural into Natural

However gloomy this plot summary may sound, *Memento Mori* is an amusing novel in Evelyn Waugh style, affirming life by showing this last stage either deepened or wasted, produced by a writer who has always been preoccupied with metaphysical questions of good and evil.

Sparks often introduces the supernatural into everyday settings as if (since the two planes co-exist side by side) sometimes the membrane between them is bound to break—a premise applied by Flannery O'Connor in her own fiction. Spark, for example, brings Satanism into the suburbs in *The Ballad of Peckham Rye*.[2] In one of her stories, as cynics are conducting a tawdry Nativity play, a real and irritable angel bursts in.

This intrusion of supernatural into natural seems, once permitted at all, to become recurrent with writers, and not simply in Frank Peretti's sagas of demonic warfare. In my novel, *Souls*

Raised from the Dead, once I had written one scene in which a possible "ghost" (the dead Miss Lila Torrido) appears while Mary Grace Thompson is dying, it became inevitable that the restless spirit of Tamsen Donner should haunt many pages of the next novel, *The Sharp Teeth of Love*, as it is inevitable that death and love are every serious writer's primary subjects. Ghosts themselves are contagious scene-stealers, appearing for example in the novels of Reynolds Price, entire story collections by Alison Lurie and Edith Wharton, in Voltaire's *Semiramis*, Henry James's *Turn of the Screw*, the work of Toni Morrison, Randall Kenan, and many other African-American writers, even as a sense of the revitalized presence of the late Joy Davidman in C.S. Lewis's *A Grief Observed*.

Whether readers decide such ghosts are actual spirits or only psychological projections matters less than the intended light that real as well as fictional death casts back onto life itself. Though one of La Rochefoucauld's maxims warns that "Death and the sun are not to be looked at steadily," Socrates did not flee Athens despite Crito's advice, and Jesus moved straight ahead to Jerusalem and Gethsemane. Jung's opinion about confronting one's own impending death is shared by Kierkegaard who— finding an advantage in our normal death-fearing despair with all its risk of meaninglessness—suggests that from that precipice man might "leap" and "fall into the open arms of God."

Two Local Deaths

On one Sunday in the spring of 1993, I was driving home from church down the narrow rutted road in Chatham County, North Carolina, that we shared with neighbors, when I was stopped by my husband's waving arms. "Frank died," he said tersely. "Can you sit with Lib till the undertaker comes?"

This couple had been our good neighbors ever since we had bought land here a decade before, land that had once been part of a larger tract owned by Lib's father. When we moved into an existing small house on those acres of pasture and forest, we must have seemed helpless city folks; but their natural kindness embraced us nonetheless, advised us on well pumps and feed dealers, sent our loose dogs home, shared garden produce.

Lib and Frank, then in their seventies, had lived through a long marriage with its good and hard times. During these later, harder days his emphysema sometimes frustrated a once active Frank; nursing him while coping with her own ailments had also made Lib weary. When his condition worsened, I served as witness on the day he signed his living will to reject extreme resuscitation measures. On that day he seemed irascible, mistrustful, as if the paper gave permission for spouse and hospice to rush him to the grave.

Now he had died at home as he preferred. I went indoors to where Lib sat like a guard by the hospital bed, watching the sheet-covered features of her husband. Although as a child I had said farewell to grandparents who then died overnight, had hugged my recuperating father only to learn by phone that he did not survive to the next dawn, had by now reached the age at which burgeoning cancers and waning hearts were killing my own former schoolmates, this was my first experience of sitting with the widow and the newly dead—a vigil that a generation earlier had been commonplace.

For an hour or so we talked about Frank, who had "died so easily," just between spoonfuls of jello being slipped into his mouth. There were memories of early marriage, golf games, other houses and jobs in other cities, baseball, their inability to have children, special vacations, his love of chocolate, and his fatal love of unfiltered cigarettes.

Gone from this history was any recollection of how illness had lately made him cross. If the dying are said in the end to review their own lives, so survivors also sort through the years, and favorably, as if the corpse might overhear. Selectively the slate is wiped clean, the sum of good increased. At one point Lib suddenly leaned forward, pulled down the sheet, and kissed Frank's cooling forehead.

Then she said softly, "I have always loved you," and covered his face again.

Afterward, in a buzz of crowded activity the undertakers came to wheel out the body, hospice workers to flush prescription pills down the commode into the septic tank, men to roll away the rented bed and oxygen equipment, until the room was suddenly empty of the whole experience. Frank would be cremated, his ashes retained until the urn eventually could be propped between Lib's embalmed hands—I do not know if this was done when she died eighteen months later.

Neither had a dramatic death; neither took a stirring nor quotable departure toward Rabelais' "great perhaps," but they had left for me a local parallel to Goethe's Baucis and Philemon, and a reminder of his words in *Elective Affinities*, "The sum which two married people owe to one another defies calculation. It is an infinite debt, which can only be charged through all eternity."

How to Die Now

Montaigne once wanted to produce a book of real and literary deaths that "in teaching men to die should after teach them to live."

In 1980, Norman and Betty Donaldson compiled the stories of three hundred real deaths in *How Did They Die?*—an alphabetical chronology stretching from Socrates to Elvis Presley.[3] Their pages primarily make readers contemplate the contrast between pre-antibiotic deathbeds at home versus today's choices between high-tech hospitals (where 50 percent of Americans died in 1949 and 80 percent do now) and Dr. Kevorkian's oxygen-stealing machine; choices among extreme unction, Elizabeth Kubler-Ross's five stages, and Raymond Moody's near-death experiences (familiarly known now as NDEs); between the mossy country churchyard and today's perpetual care parks where flat headstones make grass-cutting easy for power mowers; between those who have died accepting God's mystery and those others accepting some other metaphysic—metempsychosis, New Age karma, whatever.

During the nineteenth century, physicians encouraged to prescribe narcotics for the dying were said to engage in "obstetrics for the soul"; today lawyers and doctors more typically argue over how much more humanely we euthanize dogs and cats.

Death and Church

Let it be said straightaway that we children who grew up among Associate Reformed Presbyterians had memento mori impressed on us officially every seventh day and subliminally during nightly prayer: "if I should die before I wake." We were admonished young to work, for the night is coming, to remember our Creator in the days of our youth, and so on. Although in the Sermon on the Mount, Jesus had not one word to say about death, and although our radio heroes regularly escaped death to fight crime again in next week's sequel, Sunday school made vivid to us how Stephen went down under stones, made clear to us also that the head of John the Baptist could not be reattached.

My lifelong "remembering" since then has run the gamut. I

tried the American Society for Psychical Research, but lost patience with Ian Stevenson and those reincarnated (previously wealthy) children in India. Bridey Murphy and the Fox sisters proved fake. Every photo of ectoplasm always looked like damaged film. Even now, when insomniac, I listen to Art Bell's wee-hours broadcasts from Nevada, on which he frequently interviews time travelers, witches, UFO witnesses, Big Foot survivors, and alien abductees; but I do not phone in for details. Neither Houdini nor those whom I loved, once deceased, have ever come back bearing news. Of course kin and old friends appear in my dreams. where they always seem healed, whole, and happy while they walk along tropical beaches—but so what?

No, after transmigration and Freud's Thanatos; after the crystal balls, Ouija boards, hellfire preachers, eternal recurrence, Buddhist reabsorption, automatic writing, magnetic lees, Druid monoliths, table tipping; after Hades, Sheol, and Gehenna; beyond J.B. Rhine, Colin Wilson, Edgar Casey, Hal Lindsey, and Shirley MacLaine; after Camus' weary Sisyphus gives up; after Marcus Aurelius plus the stoicism of Ecclesiastes wears thin (these being the most appealing alternatives), there was no place for this aging Death-Rememberer to go but home to the New Testament.

Koheleth or Christ?

Ernest Becker, in his Pulitzer Prize–winning book, *The Denial of Death*, concludes, "I think it is very hard for secular men to die." He did die, of cancer, shortly after the book was published.

So did Dostoevsky die three months after finishing *The Brothers Karamazov*, which opens with a New Testament epigraph and closes with an affirmation of hope for eternal life.

Ars moriendi—the art of dying—and its parallel, the art of mourning the dead, still seem in the end to rely on secular stoicism or religious faith. For example, Sherwin B. Nuland's 1994 best seller *How We Die* is careful, scientific, even ethical; but it is not religious. And when in 1997 professional poet and also professional undertaker Thomas Lynch published his essay collection about life, death, and faith, the book was criticized in *The New York Times Book Review* from the viewpoint of a secular humanist who preferred Jessica Mitford's version.

But we Christians still meditating on the last things draw comfort when we remember that Jesus himself was no stoic on the cross. He felt despair and dread before and during the crucifixion; he cried out his challenging question to God as have King David, Job, Ivan Ilych, and millions upon millions. Stoicism is not required of believers, but hope is offered. Jane Kenyon, dead before fifty, ends one poem thus: "and God, as promised, proves / to be mercy clothed in light."

If I cannot refute the stoics, nor shrug off cosmic indifference, if I cannot cheer up Beckett's lonely characters waiting onstage, nor concur with Freud about the infantilism of religion, discard it, and then advance bravely into "hostile life," neither can these refute my sometimes wavering hope. And my emphasis is on hope, hope in God's mercy rather than fear of eternal punishment, which worried even ancient Egyptian kings and made Virgil separate the good from the justly punished dead. It is our sadism, not evangelical Christianity, that relishes medieval and hellish visions of torment, and it is our hubris that in imagination tests and tunes the personal harp and mentally tries on well-suited wings. Only if ends justify means can we (on the far side of the veil) take pleasure in separating sheep from goats forever, after we have finished (on the near side of that veil) making war on infidels and burning heretics at the stake.

Spiritual journeys into the beyond were nearly as frequent in the Middle Ages as those taken now during flat EKG moments before a defibrillator blasts the heart into rhythm again. In their context, medieval soul-travelers often saw on their journeys ample fire and brimstone; in ours the dying patient typically rushes through some final birth/death canal toward light. Doubters, of course, dismiss testimony about NDEs as a subjective response to oxygen deprivation. To them such anecdotal evidence is as unpersuasive here as in second-hand, multiple translations of Saint Paul. Even Hans Küng, in *Eternal Life*, distinguishes death as the final destination from the process leading to it, dying cell by cell, and believes most of Moody's NDE samples have experienced the first stage of that process but not the last condition.

Remember You Must Live

Memento mori, then, commands me not so much to dwell on heaven, hell, or the millennium, nor to contemplate the whole world's eventual death in apocalypse, but to value today's immediate gift of life against the backdrop of transience and God's eternity. Though Jesus acknowledged an end-time, his emphasis was on daily forgiveness and hourly love.

The earliest Gospel, Mark, takes only eleven verses to summarize all post-Resurrection events—and that is in the long version of the ending—and it ends with the Apostles at work in this world. The earliest New Testament Easter story (1 Corinthians 15) says little about the mechanics of how Christ died and then came back, but concentrates more on what his overcoming of death should mean in human lives. And that elaborator Luke, who will double everybody else's angels at every opportunity, in his Gospel relocates Jesus' ascension to Bethany but in Acts places it on Olivet. (Naturally he cannot resist adding more angels plus a spread of clouds in Acts 1:10, but the heavenly message puts a quick end to sky-gazing; clearly the coming Pentecost is more important.) And Gospel writer John shows no interest at all in post-Resurrection space travel. However original or perhaps later-appended are John's last verses, Jesus at the end of the Fourth Gospel is far too busy to take airy flight because, by patient repetition, he keeps trying to make one thing clear to Peter: "Do you love me? Feed my lambs."

Memento Which Dying, Then?

For me, as for some characters in my fiction, memento mori is an order to take life as seriously as its Creator did, to apply urgency, to view each day in an eternal context, to live right now the abundant and loving life Christ commanded—and to fail at all these but still to trust in mercy.

In addition to this heightened commitment and purpose provided by our sure mortality, I believe that in ways beyond my understanding God has in Christ defeated the former annihilating power of death.

Oh, easy to say. Too easy. Vague. Facile.

Such trust comes harder when tested against real dying. When Bob, my Early American Literature colleague in the University of North Carolina's English Department—a friend of thirty years—progressed downward by slow medical degrees from finding a lump in the groin to lymphoma, then up by way of successful chemotherapies and optimistic MRI reports, he experienced all that intensity of life measured against the risk of death. He was free to retire, to write more essays on the books he loved, to travel to Spain.

But before too long, in disguise and by sabotage, the cells in his lungs went malignant. When no more cure was available, he received at home old friends and kin and former students. There was time to laugh and talk, to share many good memories, to omit any pretense that he would long survive.

Those good times ran out. When last I came, he had turned into a skeleton thinly wrapped in yellowing pastry, eyes already closed, the breath whapping in and out with a great suck and labored release. Having been told that hearing is the last sense to shut down, I sat by this shell through which air slammed in and out, and reminded his ear of affections and blessings. It was like trying to talk to a bellows.

Next day he was gone, having told us no more about death than all the three hundred recorded in the pages of *How Did They Die?* And at the memorial service in a bland campus auditorium I swallowed hard and read aloud, as he had wished, Emily Dickinson's "Because I could not stop for Death." Cole Porter recordings were played, the Lord's Prayer murmured. By the podium Bob's color photo—pink and pre-cancer, young and already long ago—was displayed.

Not a churchgoer, Bob was perhaps not technically a Christian except in his behavior, but I have continued to remember his particular death (and the bravery by which an excellent teacher continued to teach us who would outlive him) in the context of Goethe's *Faust*. The play opens with a God-Mephistopheles wager much like the opening of Job, and it ends with Faust, who richly deserves all punishment, being granted mercy instead. When Goethe was eighty-two he emphasized that this salvation came not because it was earned but "by the divine grace vouchsafed to us."

"Say to the moment, 'Stay! Thou art so fair!' " Goethe's line captures the intensity with which we transient mortals who know we are transient must surely seize the day. And "He who strives mightily we are allowed to save," speaks to that final and mysterious grace that runs to meet all of us prodigal sons and daughters. In *Eternal Life,* Hans Küng says that Vatican II in 1964 gave hope that even atheists in good faith can attain eternal salvation.

Say to the moment, Stay! Strive mightily. Memento mori.

NOTES

1   Muriel Spark, *Memento Mori* (New York: Avon Books, 1990).

2   ———, *The Ballad of Peckham Rye* (New York: Avon Books, 1990).

3   Norman Donaldson and Betty Donaldson, *How Did They Die?* (New York: St. Martin's Press, Incorporated, 1980).

CONTRIBUTORS

RONALD AUSTIN has worked in films, television, and the theater for more than four decades. A writer, director, and producer, he has served on the Board of Directors of the Writers Guild of America, is a member of the Academy of Motion Picture Arts and Sciences and the Directors Guild, is a founding member of *Catholics in Media,* and serves on the Board of Directors of *Open Call,* the *Center for Media Literacy,* and the *Windhover Forum.* He has written film and cultural criticism for several periodicals, including the quarterly *Image: A Journal of the Arts and Religion,* and *National Catholic Register.* He currently teaches screenwriting at the University of Southern California.

SUSAN BERGMAN is Writer in Residence at Wheaton College (Illinois). Her essays and poetry have appeared widely in such publications as *Antaeus,* two Pushcart Anthologies, *Ploughshares,* and *North American Review* where she is a contributing editor. Her first book, *Anonymity,* was published in 1994. She introduced and edited *Martyrs: Contemporary Writers on Modern Lives of Faith* (1996), and is currently writing a novel, *The Buried Life.*

DAVID BOROFKA teaches English composition and literature at Kings River Community College (Reedley, California). A collection of his stories, *Hints of His Mortality,* was selected by Oscar Hijuelos as winner of the 1996 Iowa Award for short fiction; the stories in the collection have appeared in such journals as *The Southern Review, Greensboro Review,* and *Carolina Quarterly.* His first novel, *The Island,* portions of which have appeared in *Gettysburg Review* and *Shenandoah,* has just been published.

DORIS BETTS is Alumni Distinguished Professor of English at the University of North Carolina, Chapel Hill. A master of short stories as well as a novelist, poet, and essayist, she is the author of ten books, including *The Scarlet Thread* (1965), *Heading West* (1981), and *Souls Raised from the Dead* (1994). Her short stories have been published in numerous anthologies and in such magazines as *Redbook, Woman's Day,* and *The Saturday Evening Post.* Recognized in 1986 as one of three national "Master Teachers," she has been honored by the establishment of the Doris Betts Teaching Award at the University of North Carolina English Department.

RON HANSEN is the Gerard Manley Hopkins, S.J. Professor in the Arts and Humanities at Santa Clara University. His first novel, *Desperadoes* (1979) was followed by *The Assassination of Jesse James by the Coward Robert Ford,* as well as a children's book, *The Shadowmaker,* a book of stories, *Nebraska,* and his most recent novels, *Mariette in Ecstasy* and *Atticus.* A two-time recipient of fellowships from the National Endowment for the Arts and twice nominated for a PEN/Faulkner Award, he was a finalist for the National Book Award for his novel *Atticus,* and is a recipient of an Award in Literature from the American Academy and Institute of Arts and Letters.

CONTRIBUTORS

A.G. HARMON is a past recipient of The Milton Center Writing Fellowship and The Elizabeth Jones Writing Scholarship. He has been a creative writing co-mentor in The McNair Fellowship Program and was co-ordinator of the 1995 Glen Writers' Workshop. His work has appeared in publications such as *Image: A Journal of the Arts and Religion*. He has completed two novels, *In Mute Appeal* and *A House All Stilled*, and is working on a third. He holds degrees in writing and law, and is currently pursuing doctoral studies in English literature at Catholic University of America.

DEAL W. HUDSON is publisher and editor of *CRISIS*, a leading magazine of politics, culture, and the Catholic Church. He holds degrees from the University of Texas at Austin, Princeton Theological Seminary, and Emory University. He has taught at New York University, Mercer College, and Fordham University. He was a Southern Baptist minister in Atlanta for more than a decade before becoming a Catholic convert. Since coming to *CRISIS*, he has been recognized as one of the nation's leading figures in the debate over religion and culture. His work has appeared in the *Wall Street Journal*, *National Review*, and *The Washington Post*, and he has made numerous appearances on television and radio.

PHILLIP E. JOHNSON is the Jefferson E. Peyser Professor of Law at the University of California, Berkeley, where he has been a faculty member for 30 years. He is a graduate of Harvard and the University of Chicago, and served as a law clerk for Chief Justice Earl Warren of the United States Supreme Court. The author of two criminal law textbooks and of three books relating to evolution and creation, *Darwin on Trial* (1993), *Reason in the Balance* (1995), and *Defeating Darwinism—By Opening Minds* (1997), he lectures frequently in universities, churches, and elsewhere on issues relating to science, religion, and philosophy.

MADELEINE L'ENGLE has written more than 40 books of fiction and nonfiction, including one of the top ten best-selling children's books, *A Wrinkle in Time*, the 1963 winner of The Newbery Medal, *A Ring of Endless Light*, a 1980 Newbery Honor Book, and *A Ladder of Angels*, 1980 winner of the National Religious Book Award. An extensive traveler and frequent speaker, she has been awarded numerous honorary doctorates and has been honored for her contributions to literature and religion by the establishment of the L'Engle collection of her papers and manuscripts at Wheaton College (Illinois).

PAUL MARIANI is Distinguished University Professor at the University of Massachusetts, Amherst. A poet, biographer, and critic, he has authored 12 books, including five books of poetry (most recently *The Great Wheel*), studies of Hopkins and William Carlos Williams, and several biographies (most recently *Hart Crane: Making New York*). His poems have appeared in numerous anthologies as well as such journals as *Poetry, Ploughshares,* and *The Kenyon Review*. For 15 years he taught at the Bread Loaf Writers' Conference (Vermont) before serving as Dean of the Glen Eyrie Writers' Workshop in Colorado Springs. He has read his poetry throughout the U.S. and abroad, and regularly lectures on poetry and biography.

CONTRIBUTORS

ERIN MCGRAW teaches fiction writing at the University of Cincinnati. Once a Wallace Stegner Fellow in fiction at Stanford University, she is the author of two collections of short stories, *Bodies at Sea* (1989) and *Lies of the Saints* (1996). Her fiction has appeared in such magazines as *The Atlantic Monthly, The Southern Review,* and *Image: A Journal of the Arts and Religion.* She is presently completing a novel, *The Baby Tree.*

LUCI SHAW is a poet, lecturer, and retreat facilitator in church and university settings in North America and abroad, and is currently Writer in Residence at Regent College, Vancouver, Canada. Widely anthologized, she is the author of seven books of poetry, including *Polishing the Petoskey Stone* and *Writing the River,* as well as a number of non-fiction books such as *God in the Dark* and *Water My Soul: Cultivating the Interior Life.* The editor of three poetry anthologies, she has co-authored two books with Madeleine L'Engle. The past president of Harold Shaw Publishers, she is a charter member of the Chrysostom Society, a group of writers with Christian perspectives.

PAUL C. VITZ is Professor of Psychology at New York University; he is also Adjunct Professor at the John Paul II Institute for Marriage and Family, Washington, D.C., and Visiting Professor at the International Academy for Philosophy in Liechtenstein. He is the author of over 100 articles and four books, including *Psychology as Religion* (1977), *Modern Art and Modern Science: The Parallel Analysis of Vision* (1984), and *Sigmund Freud's Christian Unconscious* (1988). His work focuses on the relationship between psychology, secularism, and Christianity.

LARRY WOIWODE is the founder of the Beth-El institute for Arts and Sciences (Carson, North Dakota), where he currently teaches. A fiction writer and poet whose works have appeared in such publications as *The Atlantic Monthly, GQ, The New Yorker,* and *Paris Review,* he is the author of several books, including *What I'm Going to Do, I Think; Beyond the Bedroom Wall;* and *Poppa John.* He has been a Guggenheim fellow, and has received a William Faulkner Foundation Award (1969), a National Book Award nomination (1976), and the John Dos Passos Prize for Literature (1991). In 1995 he was named poet laureate of North Dakota and received the Award of Merit Medal from the American Academy of Arts and Letters for "distinction in the art of the short story."

HAROLD FICKETT, the editor of this book, is the author of three novels, *The Holy Fool, First Light,* and *Daybreak;* a collection of short stories, *Mrs. Sunday's Problem and Other Stories;* and a critical biography of Flannery O'Connor, *Images of Grace.* A co-founder of the quarterly *Image: A Journal of the Arts and Religion,* he served as Executive Director of The Milton Center where he administered arts programs funded by The Pew Charitable Trusts and The Lilly Endowment, Inc. From 1996 through 1997 he wrote a weekly religion column that was syndicated across North America. An active speaker in retreat and conference settings, he is currently writing a book about the parables of Jesus.